GRAMMAR
Form and Function

2A

Milada Broukal

McGraw-Hill

Published by McGraw-Hill ESL/ELT, a business unit of The McGraw-Hill Companies, Inc., 1221 Avenue of the Americas, New York, NY 10020.

ISBN: 0-07-301377-3

2 3 4 5 6 7 8 9 QPD 9 8 7 6 5 4

Editorial director: Tina B. Carver
Senior managing editor: Erik Gundersen
Developmental editors: Arley Gray, Annie Sullivan
Editorial assistants: David Averbach, Kasey Williamson
Production manager: Juanita Thompson
Cover design: AcentoVisual
Interior design: AcentoVisual
Art: Eldon Doty

Photo credits:
All photos are courtesy of Getty Images Royalty-Free Collection with the exception of the following: *Page 30* © Bettmann/CORBIS; *Page 31* © 2003 Estate of Pablo Picasso/Artists Rights Society (ARS), New York, and © Francis G. Mayer/CORBIS; *Page 34* © Hulton-Deutsch Collection/CORBIS; *Page 34* © Archivo Iconografico, S.A./CORBIS; *Page 171* © DOCWHITE.

McGraw-Hill

Contents

UNIT 1 THE PRESENT TENSES

UNIT 2 THE PAST TENSES

UNIT 3 THE FUTURE TENSES

UNIT 4 NOUNS, ARTICLES, AND QUANTITY

UNIT 5 PRONOUNS

UNIT 6 THE PERFECT TENSES

UNIT 7 QUESTIONS AND PHRASAL VERBS

APPENDICES

Acknowledgements

The publisher and author would like to thank the following individuals who reviewed *Grammar Form and Function* during the development of the series and whose comments and suggestions were invaluable in creating this project.

- Tony Albert, *Jewish Vocational Services, San Francisco, CA*
- Leslie A. Biaggi, *Miami–Dade Community College, Miami, FL*
- Gerry Boyd, *Northern Virginia Community College, VA*
- Marcia M. Captan, *Miami–Dade Community College, Miami, FL*
- Yongjae Paul Choe, *Dongguk University, Seoul, Korea*
- Sally Gearhart, *Santa Rosa Junior College, Santa Rosa, CA*
- Mary Gross, *Miramar College, San Diego, CA*
- Martin Guerin, *Miami–Dade Community College, Miami, FL*
- Patty Heiser, *University of Washington, Seattle, WA*
- Susan Kasten, *University of North Texas, Denton, TX*
- Sarah Kegley, *Georgia State University, Atlanta, GA*
- Kelly Kennedy-Isern, *Miami–Dade Community College, Miami, FL*
- Grace Low, *Germantown, TN*
- Irene Maksymjuk, *Boston University, Boston, MA*
- Christina Michaud, *Bunker Hill Community College, Boston, MA*
- Cristi Mitchell, *Miami–Dade Community College-Kendall Campus, Miami, FL*
- Carol Piñeiro, *Boston University, Boston, MA*
- Michelle Remaud, *Roxbury Community College, Boston, MA*
- Diana Renn, *Wentworth Institute of Technology, Boston, MA*
- Alice Savage, *North Harris College, Houston, TX*
- Karen Stanley, *Central Piedmont Community College, Charlotte, NC*
- Roberta Steinberg, *Mt. Ida College, Newton, MA*

The author would like to thank everyone at McGraw-Hill who participated in this project's development, especially Arley Gray, Erik Gundersen, Annie Sullivan, Jennifer Monaghan, David Averbach, Kasey Williamson, and Tina Carver.

Welcome to Grammar Form and Function!

In **Grammar Form and Function 2**, high-interest photos bring intermediate grammar to life, providing visual contexts for learning and retaining new structures and vocabulary.

Welcome to **Grammar Form and Function 2**. This visual tour will provide you with an overview of the key features of a unit.

❖ *Form* presentations teach grammar structures through complete charts and high-interest, memorable photos that facilitate students' recall of grammar structures.

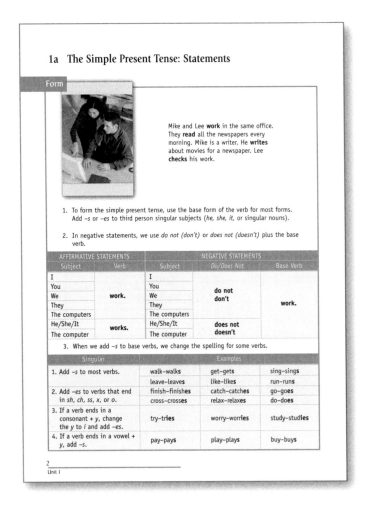

1a   The Simple Present Tense: Statements

Form

Mike and Lee **work** in the same office. They **read** all the newspapers every morning. Mike is a writer. He **writes** about movies for a newspaper. Lee **checks** his work.

1. To form the simple present tense, use the base form of the verb for most forms. Add –s or –es to third person singular subjects (*he, she, it,* or singular nouns).

2. In negative statements, we use *do not* (*don't*) or *does not* (*doesn't*) plus the base verb.

| AFFIRMATIVE STATEMENTS | | NEGATIVE STATEMENTS | | |
Subject	Verb	Subject	Do/Does Not	Base Verb
I		I		
You		You	do not	
We	work.	We	don't	
They		They		work.
The computers		The computers		
He/She/It	works.	He/She/It	does not	
The computer		The computer	doesn't	

3. When we add –s to base verbs, we change the spelling for some verbs.

Singular		Examples	
1. Add –s to most verbs.	walk–walks	get–gets	sing–sings
	leave–leaves	like–likes	run–runs
2. Add –es to verbs that end in *sh, ch, ss, x,* or *o.*	finish–finishes	catch–catches	go–goes
	cross–crosses	relax–relaxes	do–does
3. If a verb ends in a consonant + *y*, change the *y* to *i* and add –*es.*	try–tries	worry–worries	study–studies
4. If a verb ends in a vowel + *y*, add –*s.*	pay–pays	play–plays	buy–buys

2
Unit I

4. Two verbs are irregular in the simple present tense, *be* and *have*. Also, *be* forms its negative differently from other verbs.

AFFIRMATIVE STATEMENTS				NEGATIVE STATEMENTS		
	Subject	Verb		Subject	Negative Verb	
Be	I	am	late.	I	am not 'm not	late.
	You We They	are		You We They	are not 're not aren't	
	He/She/It	is		He/She/It	is not 's not isn't	
Have	I You We They	have	a problem.	I You We They	don't have	a problem.
	He/She/It	has		He/She/It	doesn't have	

Function

1. We use the simple present tense when we talk about habitual actions and for things that happen all the time or are always true.

   Mike **talks** on the phone a lot.
   He **writes** movie reviews on his computer every day.

2. We use the negative contracted forms *don't* and *doesn't* in speech and informal writing. We use the full forms *do not* and *does not* in formal writing and in speech when we want to emphasize the negative.

   INFORMAL: I'm sorry. I **don't** have time to help you now.
   FORMAL OR EMPHATIC: The president **does not** want this report to be late.

3
The Present Tenses

❖ *Form* presentations also include related grammatical points such as negatives, yes/no questions, wh– questions, and short answers.

❖ *Function* explanations and examples clarify when to use grammar structures.

---

1 Practice

Complete the sentences with the correct form of the verb in parentheses. Make the verb negative if the word *not* is in the parentheses.

1. Mike (live) _____*lives*_____ in New York City.
2. He (have) _____ an apartment near the office.
3. He (not, take) _____ the bus to work.
4. He (walk) _____ to work.
5. Mike (like) _____ his job.
6. He (not, be) _____ an office worker.
7. He (be) _____ a writer.
8. He (write) _____ about movies.
9. He (go) _____ to the movies every day.
10. He (see) _____ new movies.
11. He (have) _____ a small computer.
12. He (take) _____ his computer with him to the movies.
13. He (not, go) _____ home at 5:00 in the afternoon.
14. Mike (work) _____ late.
15. He (sleep) _____ late, too.
16. Lee (correct) _____ his work.
17. They (work) _____ for the same newspaper.
18. Mike and Lee (read) _____ a lot of other newspapers.
19. They (talk) _____ on the phone a lot.
20. They (drink) _____ a lot of coffee, too.
21. Mike and Lee (not, agree) _____ all the time.
22. Lee (not, like) _____ Mike's work all the time.

2 Your Turn

Think of five activities that a friend does. Tell your partner.

Examples:
My sister teaches art to children.
She drives to work.
She helps the children.
She likes her job.

4
Unit 1

❖ **Extensive practice** through topical exercises guides students from accurate production to fluent use of the grammar.

❖ **Your Turn** activities guide students to practice grammar in personally meaningful conversations.

❖ **Writing assignments build composition skills, such as narrating and describing, through real-life, step-by-step tasks.**

WRITING: Describe a Person

Write a paragraph about your partner.

Step 1. Ask and answer the questions with a partner. Record the answers by checking "Yes" or "No." Write additional information under "Other Information."

	Yes	No	Other Information
1. live/in (city)	_____	_____	_____
2. work	_____	_____	_____
3. like/tennis	_____	_____	_____
4. listen/pop music	_____	_____	_____
5. have/car	_____	_____	_____
6. go/movies on weekends	_____	_____	_____
7. speak/(language)	_____	_____	_____
8. play/the piano	_____	_____	_____
9. go on vacation/in the summer	_____	_____	_____
10. have/brothers and sisters	_____	_____	_____

Step 2. Write sentences about your partner from your notes.

Example:
Kumiko lives in Tokyo.
She doesn't work.
She goes to school.

Step 3. Rewrite the sentences in the form of a paragraph. Write a title (your partner's name). For more writing guidelines, see pages 410–416.

Kumiko Osawa

Kumiko lives in Tokyo She doesn't work because she's a student. She likes...

Step 4. Evaluate your paragraph.

Checklist
_____ Did you indent the first line?
_____ Did you give the paragraph a title?
_____ Did you write the title with a capital letter for each word?

Step 5. Edit your work. Work with a partner or your teacher to edit your sentences. Correct spelling, punctuation, vocabulary, and grammar.

Step 6. Write your final copy.

SELF-TEST

A Choose the best answer, A, B, C, or D, to complete the sentence. Mark your answer by darkening the oval with the same letter.

1. Many animals _____ their young in the spring.

   A. are having   Ⓐ Ⓑ Ⓒ Ⓓ
   B. have
   C. has
   D. is have

2. Every year, the Earth _____ around the Sun one time.

   A. travels   Ⓐ Ⓑ Ⓒ Ⓓ
   B. travel
   C. is traveling
   D. does traveling

3. Snow _____ in the Sahara Desert.

   A. sometimes falls   Ⓐ Ⓑ Ⓒ Ⓓ
   B. sometimes is falling
   C. falls sometimes
   D. is falling sometimes

4. Sharks _____ bones.

   A. do not have   Ⓐ Ⓑ Ⓒ Ⓓ
   B. are not having
   C. have not

6. At the moment, everybody _____ the football game on television.

   A. is seeing   Ⓐ Ⓑ Ⓒ Ⓓ
   B. is watching
   C. is looking at
   D. does watch

7. We _____ vitamins for good health.

   A. are needing   Ⓐ Ⓑ Ⓒ Ⓓ
   B. need have
   C. have need
   D. need

8. Young children _____ the pictures in books.

   A. always look at   Ⓐ Ⓑ Ⓒ Ⓓ
   B. always see
   C. look at always
   D. always watch

9. When _____ breakfast?

   A. you have   Ⓐ Ⓑ Ⓒ Ⓓ
   B. have you
   C. do you have

❖ **Self-Tests** at the end of each unit allow students to evaluate their mastery of the grammar while providing informal practice of standardized test taking.

B Find the underlined word or phrase, A, B, C, or D, that is incorrect. Mark your answer by darkening the oval with the same letter.

1. Italians <u>usually</u> <u>eats</u> pasta <u>every day</u>
       A   B   C

   <u>of the week</u>.
   D

   Ⓐ Ⓑ Ⓒ Ⓓ

2. <u>How many</u> <u>hours</u> does <u>a baby</u> <u>sleeps</u>?
     A   B   C   D

   Ⓐ Ⓑ Ⓒ Ⓓ

3. <u>People</u> catch <u>sometimes</u> <u>colds</u> <u>in the</u> winter.
     A   B   C   D

   Ⓐ Ⓑ Ⓒ Ⓓ

4. <u>Do</u> bears <u>eat</u> only meat, or <u>they do</u> <u>eat</u>
     A   B   C   D
   plants, too?

   Ⓐ Ⓑ Ⓒ Ⓓ

6. In India, the cow <u>gives</u> <u>milk</u> <u>and</u>
                   A   B   C

   <u>is working</u> on the farm.
   D

   Ⓐ Ⓑ Ⓒ Ⓓ

7. Camels <u>do not</u> <u>drink</u> <u>often</u> water for days
           A   B   C
   when they <u>travel</u>.
             D

   Ⓐ Ⓑ Ⓒ Ⓓ

8. When <u>do</u> people <u>use</u> computers, they
         A   B
   <u>often</u> <u>use</u> the Internet to get information.
   C   D

   Ⓐ Ⓑ Ⓒ Ⓓ

9. <u>Men and women</u> in Iceland <u>have</u> long lives
           A   B
   because the air <u>has</u> clean and they <u>have</u>

To the Teacher

Grammar Form and Function is a three-level series designed to ensure students' success in learning grammar. The series features interesting photos to help students accurately recall grammar points, meaningful contexts, and a clear, easy-to-understand format that integrates practice of the rules of essential English grammar (form) with information about when to apply them and what they mean (function).

Features

❖ **Flexible approach to grammar instruction** integrates study of new structures (form) with information on how to use them and what they mean (function).
❖ **High-interest photos** contextualize new grammar and vocabulary.
❖ **Comprehensive grammar coverage** targets all intermediate structures.
❖ **Extensive practice** ensures accurate production and fluent use of grammar.
❖ **Your Turn activities** guide students to practice grammar in personally meaningful conversations.
❖ **Writing assignments** build composition skills like narrating and describing through step-by-step tasks.
❖ **Self-Tests and Unit Quizzes** offer multiple assessment tools for student and teacher use, in print and Web formats.
❖ **Companion Website activities** develop real-world listening and reading skills.

Components

❖ **Student Book** has 14 units with abundant practice in both form and function of each grammar structure. Each unit also features communicative *Your Turn* activities, a step-by-step *Writing* assignment, and a *Self-Test*.
❖ **Teacher's Manual** provides the following:
   ◆ Teaching tips and techniques
   ◆ Overview of each unit
   ◆ Answer keys for the Student Book and Workbook
   ◆ Expansion activities
   ◆ Culture, usage, and vocabulary notes
   ◆ Answers to frequently asked questions about the grammar structures
   ◆ Unit quizzes in a standardized test format and answer keys for each unit.
❖ **Workbook** features additional exercises for each grammar structure, plus an extra student Self-Test at the end of each unit.
❖ **Website** provides further practice, as well as additional assessments.

Overview of the Series
Pedagogical Approach

What is *form*?

Form is the structure of a grammar point and what it looks like. Practice of the form builds students' accuracy and helps them recognize the grammar point in authentic situations, so they are better prepared to understand what they are reading or what other people are saying.

What is *function*?

Function is when and how we use a grammar point. Practice of the function builds students' fluency and helps them apply the grammar point in their real lives.

Why does **Grammar Form and Function** incorporate both form and function into its approach to teaching grammar?

Mastery of grammar relies on students knowing the rules of English (form) and correctly understanding how to apply them (function). Providing abundant practice in both form and function is key to student success.

How does **Grammar Form and Function** incorporate form and function into its approach to teaching grammar?

For each grammar point, the text follows a consistent format:

❖ **Presentation of Form.** The text presents the complete form, or formal rule, along with several examples for students to clearly see the model. There are also relevant photos to help illustrate the grammar point.

❖ **Presentation of Function.** The text explains the function of the grammar point, or how it is used, along with additional examples for reinforcement.

❖ **Practice.** Diverse exercises practice the form and function together. Practice moves logically from more controlled to less controlled activities.

❖ **Application.** Students apply the grammar point in open-ended communicative activities. **Your Turn** requires students to draw from and speak about personal experiences, and **Writing** provides a variety of writing assignments that rely on communicative group and pair discussions. **Expansion** activities in the Teacher's Manual provide additional creative, fun practice for students.

What is the purpose of the photos in the book?

Most people have a visual memory. When you see a photo aligned with a grammar point, the photo helps you remember and contextualize the grammar. The photo reinforces the learning and retention. If there were no visual image, you'd be more likely to forget the grammar point. For example, let's say you are learning the present progressive. You read the example "She is drinking a glass of water." At the same time, you are shown a photo of a girl drinking a glass of water. Later, you are more likely to recall the form of the present progressive because your mind has made a mental picture that helps you remember.

Practice

How were the grammar points selected?

We did a comprehensive review of courses at this level to ensure that all of the grammar points taught were included.

Does **Grammar Form and Function** have controlled or communicative practice?

It has both. Students practice each grammar point through controlled exercises and then move on to tackle open-ended communicative activities.

Do students have a chance to personalize the grammar?

Yes. There are opportunities to personalize the grammar in **Your Turn** and **Writing**. **Your Turn** requires students to draw from and speak about personal experiences, and **Writing** provides a variety of writing assignments that rely on communicative group and pair discussions.

Does **Grammar Form and Function** help students work toward fluency or accuracy?

Both. The exercises are purposefully designed to increase students' accuracy and enhance their fluency by practicing both form and function. Students' confidence in their accuracy helps boost their fluency.

Why does the text feature writing practice?

Grammar and writing are linked in a natural way. Specific grammar structures lend themselves to specific writing genres. In *Grammar Form and Function*, carefully devised practice helps students keep these structures in mind as they are writing.

In addition to the grammar charts, what other learning aids are in the book?

The book includes 11 pages of appendices that are designed to help the students as they complete the exercises. In addition to grammar resources such as lists of irregular verbs and spelling rules for endings, the appendices also feature useful and interesting information, including grammar terms, rules for capitalization and punctuation, writing basics, and even maps. In effect, the appendices constitute a handbook that students can use not only in grammar class, but in other classes as well.

Are there any additional practice opportunities?

Yes, there are additional exercises in the Workbook and on the Website. There are also **Expansion** activities in the Teacher's Manual that provide more open-ended (and fun!) practice for students.

Assessment

What is the role of student self-assessment in Grammar Form and Function?

Every opportunity for student self-assessment is valuable! *Grammar Form and Function* provides two Self-Tests for each unit – one at the end of each Student Book unit and another at the end of each Workbook unit. The Self-Tests build student confidence, encourage student independence as learners, and increase student competence in following standardized test formats. In addition, the Self-Tests serve as important tools for the teacher in measuring student mastery of grammar structures.

Does Grammar Form and Function offer students practice in standardized test formats?

Yes, the two Self-Tests and the Unit Quiz for each unit all utilize standardized test formats. Teachers may use the three tests in the way that best meets student, teacher, and institutional needs. For example, teachers may first assign the Self-Test in the Workbook as an untimed practice test to be taken at home. Then in the classroom, teachers may administer the Self-Test in the Student Book for a more realistic, but still informal, test-taking experience. Finally, teachers may administer the Unit Quiz from the Teacher's Manual as a more standardized timed test.

How long should each Self-Test or Unit Quiz take?

Since there is flexibility in implementing the Self-Tests and Unit Quizzes, there is also flexibility in the timing of the tests. When used for informal test-taking practice at home or in class, they may be administered as untimed tests. When administered as timed tests in class, they should take no more than 20 minutes.

How can I be sure students have mastered the grammar?

Grammar Form and Function provides a variety of tools to evaluate student mastery of the grammar. Traditional evaluation tools include the practice exercises, Self-Tests, and Unit Quizzes. To present a more complete picture of student mastery, the series also includes **Your Turn** activities and **Writing**, which illustrate how well students have internalized the grammar structures and are able to apply them in realistic tasks. Teachers can use these activities to monitor and assess students' ability to incorporate new grammatical structures into their spoken and written discourse.

Unit Format

What is the unit structure of Grammar Form and Function?

Consult the guide to *Grammar Form and Function* on pages VII-X. This walkthrough provides a visual tour of a Student Book unit.

How many hours of instruction are in Grammar Form and Function 2?

The key to *Grammar Form and Function* is flexibility! The grammar structures in the Student Book may be taught in order, or teachers may rearrange units into an order that best meets their students' needs. To shorten the number of hours of instruction, teachers may choose not to teach all of the grammar structures, or use all of the exercises provided. On the other hand, teachers may add additional hours by assigning exercises in the Workbook or on the Website. In addition, the Teacher's Manual provides teaching suggestions and expansion activities that would add extra hours of instruction.

Ancillary Components

What can I find in the Teacher's Manual?

* Teaching tips and techniques
* Overview of each unit
* Answer keys for the Student Book and Workbook
* Expansion activities
* Culture, usage, and vocabulary notes
* Answers to frequently asked questions about the grammar structures
* Unit quizzes in a standardized test format and quiz answer keys.

How do I supplement classroom instruction with the Workbook?

The Workbook exercises can be used to add instructional hours to the course, to provide homework practice, and to reinforce and refresh the skills of students who have mastered the grammar structures. It also provides additional standardized test-taking practice.

What can students find on the Website?

Students and teachers will find a wealth of engaging listening and reading activities on the *Grammar Form and Function* Website. As with the Workbook, the Website exercises can be used to add instructional hours to the course, to provide homework practice, and to reinforce and refresh the skills of students who have mastered the grammar structures.

UNIT 1

THE PRESENT TENSES

1a   The Simple Present Tense: Statements

1b   Adverbs of Frequency

1c   The Present Progressive Tense: Statements

1d   The Simple Present Tense OR The Present Progressive Tense
(**I work.** OR **I am working.**)

1e   Nonprogressive Verbs (**I think.** OR **I am thinking.**)

1f   *See, Look At, Watch, Hear,* and *Listen To*

1g   Yes/No Questions and Short Answers; Wh- Questions

❖   Writing

❖   Self-Test

1a   The Simple Present Tense: Statements

Mike and Lee **work** in the same office. They **read** all the newspapers every morning. Mike is a writer. He **writes** about movies for a newspaper. Lee **checks** his work.

1. To form the simple present tense, use the base form of the verb for most forms. Add *–s* or *–es* to third person singular subjects (*he, she, it,* or singular nouns).

2. In negative statements, we use *do not (don't)* or *does not (doesn't)* plus the base verb.

AFFIRMATIVE STATEMENTS		NEGATIVE STATEMENTS		
Subject	Verb	Subject	*Do/Does Not*	Base Verb
I		I		
You		You	do not	
We	work.	We	don't	
They		They		work.
The computers		The computers		
He/She/It	works.	He/She/It	does not	
The computer		The computer	doesn't	

3. When we add *–s* to base verbs, we change the spelling for some verbs.

Singular	Examples		
1. Add *–s* to most verbs.	walk–walk**s**	get–get**s**	sing–sing**s**
	leave–leave**s**	like–like**s**	run–run**s**
2. Add *–es* to verbs that end in *sh, ch, ss, x,* or *o.*	finish–finish**es**	catch–catch**es**	go–go**es**
	cross–cross**es**	relax–relax**es**	do–do**es**
3. If a verb ends in a consonant + *y,* change the *y* to *i* and add *–es.*	try–tr**ies**	worry–worr**ies**	study–stud**ies**
4. If a verb ends in a vowel + *y,* add *–s.*	pay–pay**s**	play–play**s**	buy–buy**s**

4. Two verbs are irregular in the simple present tense, *be* and *have*. Also, *be* forms its negative differently from other verbs.

	AFFIRMATIVE STATEMENTS			NEGATIVE STATEMENTS		
	Subject	Verb		Subject	Negative Verb	
Be	I	**am**	late.	I	**am not** **'m not**	late.
	You We They	**are**		You We They	**are not** **'re not** **aren't**	
	He/She/It	**is**		He/She/It	**is not** **'s not** **isn't**	
Have	I You We They	**have**	a problem.	I You We They	**don't have**	a problem.
	He/She/It	**has**		He/She/It	**doesn't have**	

1. We use the simple present tense when we talk about habitual actions and for things that happen all the time or are always true.

> Mike **talks** on the phone a lot.
> He **writes** movie reviews on his computer every day.

2. We use the negative contracted forms *don't* and *doesn't* in speech and informal writing. We use the full forms *do not* and *does not* in formal writing and in speech when we want to emphasize the negative.

> INFORMAL: I'm sorry. I **don't** have time to help you now.
> FORMAL OR EMPHATIC: The president **does not** want this report to be late.

1 Practice

Complete the sentences with the correct form of the verb in parentheses. Make the verb negative if the word *not* is in the parentheses.

1. Mike (live) _____*lives*_____ in New York City.
2. He (have) _____ an apartment near the office.
3. He (not, take) _____ the bus to work.
4. He (walk) _____ to work.
5. Mike (like) _____ his job.
6. He (not, be) _____ an office worker.
7. He (be) _____ a writer.
8. He (write) _____ about movies.
9. He (go) _____ to the movies every day.
10. He (see) _____ new movies.
11. He (have) _____ a small computer.
12. He (take) _____ his computer with him to the movies.
13. He (not, go) _____ home at 5:00 in the afternoon.
14. Mike (work) _____ late.
15. He (sleep) _____ late, too.
16. Lee (correct) _____ his work.
17. They (work) _____ for the same newspaper.
18. Mike and Lee (read) _____ a lot of other newspapers.
19. They (talk) _____ on the phone a lot.
20. They (drink) _____ a lot of coffee, too.
21. Mike and Lee (not, agree) _____ all the time.
22. Lee (not, like) _____ Mike's work all the time.

2 Your Turn

Think of five activities that a friend does. Tell your partner.

Example:
My sister teaches art to children.
She drives to work.
She helps the children.
She likes her job.
She sees a movie every weekend.

3 | Your Turn

Think of four things you do every day and four things you don't do every day. List them here, and then talk about them with a partner.

Examples:
I exercise every day.
I don't cook every day.

Things I do every day:

1. _____

2. _____

3. _____

4. _____

Things I don't do every day:

5. _____

6. _____

7. _____

8. _____

4 | Practice

Complete the sentences with the _–s_ or _–es_ spelling of the verb in parentheses.

1. John (get up) _____*gets up*_____ at noon.

2. He (eat) _____ breakfast.

3. He (watch) _____ television.

4. He (meet) _____ his friends.

5. He (eat) _____ lunch.

6. He (try) _____ to find a job.

7. He (listen) _____ to music with his friends.

8. In the evening, he (eat) _____ dinner in a restaurant.

9. He (go out) _____ with his friends.

10. John (come) _____ home at four o'clock in the morning.

11. On Sundays, he (stay) _____ home.

12. He (wash) _____ his clothes.

13. He (clean) _____ his apartment.

14. He (fix) _____ things in the apartment.

15. He (relax) _____.

16. He (call) _____ his mother.

17. His mother (worry) _____ about him.

5 │ What Do You Think?

Why does John's mother worry about him?

6 │ Practice

Work with a partner. Tell your partner what each of the people below do.

Example:
A mechanic fixes cars.

doctor   mechanic   teacher   painter   chef

1b Adverbs of Frequency

Form

This is Ann Philips.
She's a host on morning television.
We **often** see her on "Good Morning."
She **always** gets up early on workdays.
She **usually** arrives at the studio at 4:30 in the morning.

Never, rarely, seldom, sometimes, often, usually, and *always* are adverbs of frequency. They come between the subject and the simple present verb.

0%					100%
never	**rarely** **seldom**	**sometimes**	**often**	**usually**	**always**

Subject	Adverb of Frequency	Simple Present Tense	
I	**never**	**eat**	Chinese food.
You	**rarely**	**go**	to the theater.
He	**seldom**	**sees**	friends.
She	**sometimes**	**drinks**	tea.
It	**often**	**snows**	in winter.
We	**usually**	**get up**	early.
They	**always**	**have**	breakfast.

Function

Adverbs of frequency tell us how often something happens.

Ann **always** starts the show at 7:00 in the morning.
She **never** gets angry on the show.
She **usually** smiles a lot on the show.

7 Practice

Rewrite the sentences and put the adverbs in the correct position.

1. On workdays, I get up at 3:30 in the morning.

   (always) *From Monday to Friday, I always get up at 3:30 in the morning.*

2. I take a shower.

   (always) _____

3. I leave the house at 4:15.

   (usually) _____

4. I get to the studio at 4:30.

   (usually) _____

5. "Good Morning" starts at 7:00.

   (always) _____

6. I leave the studio at 10:00.

   (usually) _____

7. I go to the gym after work.

   (usually) _____

8. I go shopping after the gym.

   (sometimes) _____

9. My husband comes home at 7:30 in the evening.

(usually) _____

10. We stay home in the evening.

(always) _____

11. We go out on weekdays.

(sometimes) _____

12. We watch television.

(often) _____

13. I go to bed at 9:00.

(usually) _____

14. On weekends, I get up before 10:00 in the morning.

(rarely) _____

15. We see friends.

(often) _____

16. We go to the movies.

(never) _____

17. I get up early on Monday.

(always) _____

8 Practice

Work with a partner. Talk about Ann's life.

Example:
Ann always gets up early on weekdays.

9 Your Turn

Which of these do you always do, sometimes do, or never do during the week?

Example:
I always cook dinner, and I usually do my homework.

cook dinner	go to school	have lunch	see friends
do my homework	go to the movies	play football	watch television

1c The Present Progressive Tense: Statements

People **are walking** to their gates.
They **are carrying** suitcases.

1. We form the present progressive tense with a present form of *be* (*am, is,* or *are*) + the *–ing* form of a verb.

AFFIRMATIVE AND NEGATIVE STATEMENTS			
Subject	Form of *Be*	*(Not)*	Verb + *–ing*
I	**am**		
You	**are**		
He/She/it	**is**	**(not)**	**working.**
We	**are**		
They			

FULL FORMS	CONTRACTIONS	
Full Form	Subject + Form of *Be*	Form of *Be* + *Not*
I am (not)	I'm (not)	*
You are (not)	You're (not)	You aren't
He/She/ It is (not)	He's (not)	He isn't
	She's (not)	She isn't
	It's (not)	It isn't
We are (not)	We're (not)	We aren't
They are (not)	They're (not)	They aren't

*There is no contraction for *am not*.

2. When we add *–ing* to a base verb, we change the spelling for some verbs.

Base Verb Ending	Rule	Example	
For most verb endings	Add *–ing*	start	start**ing**
		play	play**ing**
		study	study**ing**
The verb ends in a consonant + *e*.	Drop *e*, add *–ing*.	live	liv**ing**
		move	mov**ing**
		decide	decid**ing**
The verb ends in a single vowel + a consonant.	Double the consonant, add *–ing*.	stop	stop**ping**
		plan	plan**ning**
		prefer	prefer**ring**
Exceptions: Do not double *w* or *x*.		fix	fix**ing**
		show	show**ing**
If a verb has two or more syllables and the stress is not on the last syllable, do not double the consonant.		open	open**ing**
		travel	travel**ing**
		exit	exit**ing**
The verb ends in *ie*.	Change *ie* to *y* and add *–ing*.	tie	tying
		die	dying

A man **is standing** next to a bench.
He **is wearing** a coat.
They are waiting at the airport.

1. We use the present progressive to talk about what is happening *now*.

2. We use contractions in speech and in informal writing. We use full forms in formal writing and when we want to give emphasis to what we are saying.

10 Practice

Write the *–ing* forms of the verbs.

Base Verb	Verb + *–ing*
1. listen	*listening*
2. wait	_____
3. study	_____
4. die	_____
5. stay	_____
6. admit	_____
7. swim	_____
8. choose	_____
9. write	_____
10. cut	_____
11. sleep	_____
12. rain	_____
13. start	_____
14. hit	_____
15. happen	_____
16. begin	_____
17. win	_____
18. tie	_____
19. open	_____
20. hope	_____

11 Practice

Complete the sentences with the present progressive tense of the verb in parentheses.

I love airports. At the moment, I (wait) _____ *am waiting* _____ for my plane.
                                              1

I have three hours. So what am I doing? I (not, sleep) _____!
                                                                2

I (watch) _____ people. Look at that man. He's outside the
                    3

bookstore. He (carry) _____ a big black bag. He
                              4

(look) _____ around. He (walk) _____
                5   6

away now. He (not, smile) _____. He looks worried. Now he
                                    7

(go) _____ to the departure gate. Here comes a woman. She
           8

(not, walk) _____ . She (run) _____
               9   **10**

after the man. She (hold) _____ a passport in her hand.
                              11

She (shout) _____ something. The man
                 12

(turn) _____ , and now he (smile) _____ .
          13   **14**

The woman (wave) _____ her hand with the passport. He
                     15

(put) _____ his arm around her now. They look happy.
         16

12 Practice

Test your memory. Work with a partner. Make three true statements and three false statements about the photo on page 9. Your partner tells you if they are true or false without looking at the photo.

Example:
You: The people are sitting down.
Your partner: That's false.

13 Your Turn

Describe two of the people in the photo on page 10. Write three sentences about what they are wearing and what they are doing.

Example:
The man on the right is sitting down.

Person 1

1. _____

_____

2. _____

_____

3. _____

_____

Person 2

1. _____

_____

2. _____

_____

3. _____

_____

1d The Simple Present Tense OR The Present Progressive Tense

Charlie always **starts** work at nine.
Charlie **loves** his job.

Today, Charlie **isn't working**.
Charlie **is staying** in bed.

We use the simple present tense for:	We use the present progressive tense for:

1. Repeated actions or habits.
 	
    Charlie **gets up** at 7:00 every day.
	1. Things that are happening now.
	
	    He **is trying** to sleep.

2. Things that happen all the time or are always true.
 	
    He always **stays** home when he's sick.
    He **gets** tired when he works too much.	

14 Practice

Complete the conversation with the correct form of the present progressive or the simple present of the verb in parentheses.

Detective Roberts is watching a house. He's talking to Detective Jason on his cell phone.

Detective Roberts: An old woman (come) _____*is coming*_____ out of the

                     house.
                                                    1

Detective Jason: That's Mrs. Johnson. She (live) _____

                     there. She's the housekeeper. It's 8:00 o'clock. She usually
                                                    2

(leave) _____ the house at 8:00. She

             3

(go) _____ to the store to do the grocery

       4

shopping. She usually (come) _____ back

                    5

around 9:30.

Detective Roberts: Wait! A car (stop) _____ in front of the house.

                           6

A man (get) _____ out. He is tall and thin

                7

and has gray hair. He (wear) _____ a uniform.

                    8

Detective Jason: I know he (not, live) _____ there.

                    9

Detective Roberts: He (ring) _____ the doorbell.

              10

Nobody (answer) _____ . He

              11

(wait) _____ now. He

       12

(look) _____ at the house carefully. He

       13

(go) _____ to the back of the house. He

     14

(jump) _____ over the wall.

       15

Detective Jason: Go get him, Roberts!

Detective Roberts runs after the man and then returns to his car.

Detective Roberts: No luck. He says he (look) _____ for the gas

                      16

meter. He is from the gas company. He has a badge.

15   Practice

Solve the riddles. Complete the sentences with the correct form of the verb in parentheses. At the end of each paragraph, identify the thing that the paragraph describes.

A.

I usually (stand) _____*stand*_____ in the kitchen. I

            1

(have) _____ a door. People (open) _____

     2   **3**

the door and (put) _____ things inside me. Part of me

              4

(freeze) _____ things for people. Right now, a woman

       5

(take) _____ out a bottle of cold water.

     6

What am I? _____ .

       7

B.

You (find) _____ me in the kitchen or bathroom.
                 1

You probably (use) _____ me every day. You
                        2

(use) _____ me to clean things. Right now, I am in
        3

the kitchen sink. Someone (rub) _____ me all over a pot.
                                    4

What am I? _____ .
                  5

C.

I (have) _____ six legs. I (fly) _____
              1   2

around in rooms. I (live) _____ in warm weather. Some people
                              3

(not, like) _____ me. Right now, I
                4

(sit) _____ on a window. I (try) _____
          5   6

to get out. A man (come) _____ toward me. He has a rolled up
                              7

newspaper in his hand.

What am I? _____ .
                  8

1e Nonprogressive Verbs

Timmy **wants** a cookie.
He **loves** chocolate cookies.
Right now, he**'s thinking** about eating one.

1. We do not usually use some verbs in the present progressive tense. We call these *nonprogressive verbs*.

CORRECT:	That cake **tastes** good.
INCORRECT:	That cake ~~is tasting~~ good.

CORRECT:	Shirley **wants** a sandwich.
INCORRECT:	Shirley ~~is wanting~~ a sandwich.

Common Nonprogressive Verbs			
be	hate	love	smell
believe	have	need	taste
enjoy	hear	prefer	think
feel	know	remember	understand
forget	like	see	want

2. Sometimes we use the verbs *have* and *think* in the present progressive tense.

Verb	Example	Explanation
Think	He **thinks** it is a good idea.	*Thinks* means *believes*.
	He **is thinking** about eating a cookie.	*Is thinking* refers to the thoughts going through his mind.
Have	Shirley **has** a cell phone.	*Have* means *possess*.
	She's **having** a good time.	You can use *have* in the present progressive in certain idiomatic expressions: **have a good/bad time** **have problems/difficulty** **have breakfast/lunch/dinner** You can also use the simple present with these expressions. Compare: She always **has** a good time at parties. Look at her dance! She's **having** a good time.

16 Practice

Complete the letter with the simple present or the present progressive of the verbs in parentheses.

Dear Pete,

I (write) _____*am writing*_____ to you from Sandy Beach, California. I am here
                                1

with Kate and Sally. We (stay) _____ at my friend Brenda's house.
                                                    2

She (have) _____ a beautiful house by the beach here. She

(come) _____ here every summer.

We (have) _____ a good time. Every morning, we

(go) _____ to the beach, and we (swim) _____.

At noon, we (come) _____ back to the house and

(have) _____ lunch. We (rest) _____

in the afternoon, and then we (go) _____ into town. We

(sit) _____ in a café or (eat) _____ dinner

in a restaurant.

Today, it (rain) _____. We (stay) _____

at home. I (not, like) _____ this weather. Kate and Sally

(watch) _____ videos. Brenda (cook) _____

lunch for us. It (smell) _____ good.

I hope to see you soon.

Love,
Annie

1f   *See, Look At, Watch, Hear,* and *Listen To*

She **is listening to** music.

The children **are watching** television.

One man **is looking at** his watch.

1. We use several verbs to express the senses of seeing and hearing. They are different from each other in meaning and in the tenses that we use with them.

VERBS OF SEEING			
	Verb	Meaning	Example
Action Verbs	watch	We *watch* something or someone that is moving. We usually *watch* something that we are paying attention to.	Charles **is watching** television. He **watches** television every evening.
	look at	We *look at* something or someone for a reason.	Susan **is looking at** a painting. She is an art student. She **looks at** paintings carefully.
Nonaction Verb	see	We *see* things because our eyes are open.	I **see** the blackboard at the front of the room.

VERBS OF HEARING			
	Verb	Meaning	Example
Action Verb	listen to	We *listen to* something or someone for a reason.	They **are listening to** music. They **listen to** music often.
Nonaction Verb	hear	When we *hear,* we receive sounds with our ears.	I **hear** the music coming from the other room. (I may not be paying attention to it.)

2. We can use action verbs either with the simple present tense or with the present progressive tense. But we do not usually use nonaction verbs with the present progressive tense.

17 Practice

Complete the sentences with the correct verb. Use the simple present or the present progressive tense.

1. Right now the students (listen to/hear) _____*are listening to*_____ the teacher. She is teaching the present progressive.

2. Tommy (watch/look at) _____ a football game on television right now.

3. Susan (watch/look at) _____ her watch. She wants to know what time it is.

4. The teacher (look at/see) _____ Bob. She is waiting for an answer to her question.

5. I am studying in my room, but I (hear/listen to) _____ the television in the next room.

6. I (look at/see) _____ the teacher so I can understand better.

7. Tony (listen to/hear) _____ Susan carefully. She is giving him directions to the bank.

8. Dick turns on the television and (watch/see) _____ the news every morning at 7:00.

9. It is 11:00 at night. Tim is in bed. He (hear/listen to) _____ a noise in his apartment. He gets up. He (see/look at) _____ his cat on the kitchen table.

10. Mary is eating soup in a restaurant. She looks down and (see/look at) _____ a hair in the soup. She calls the waiter.

11. (hear/listen to) _____ that sound! I think someone is trying to get in!

12. Brenda is only four years old. She likes magazines. She can't read, but she (look at/see) _____ the photos.

18 | Your Turn

Ask and answer the questions with a partner.

Example:
You: What are you looking at right now? What do you see?
Your partner: I'm looking out the window. I see buildings and students.

1. What are you looking at right now? What do you see?
2. What are you listening to right now? What do you hear?
3. What do you like to watch on television?

1g Yes/No Questions and Short Answers; Wh- Questions

Woman:	**Are you waiting** for the flight to London at 10:00?
Man:	**Yes, I am.** Do you live in London?
Woman:	**No, I don't.** I live in Montreal. **Where do** you **live**?
Man:	I live in Singapore.

1. Yes/No questions are questions that we can answer with the words *yes* or *no*.

2. Wh- questions begin with a question word like *who* or *what*. We call them wh- questions because all except one begin with the letters *wh-*. The question words are *who, whom, what, where, when, why, which,* and *how*.

	YES/NO QUESTIONS			SHORT ANSWERS
	Do/Does	Subject	Base Verb	
Simple Present	**Do**	I	**need** a haircut?	Yes, you **do.** No, you **don't.**
		you		Yes, I/we **do.** No, I/we **don't.**
		we		Yes, you **do.** No, you **don't.**
		they		Yes, they **do.** No, they **don't.**
	Does	he/she/it		Yes, he/she/it **does.** No, he/she/it **doesn't.**

YES/NO QUESTIONS				SHORT ANSWERS
	Am/Is/Are	Subject	Verb + *–ing*	
Present Progressive	**Am**	I	**leaving** now?	Yes, you **are.** No, you **aren't.** OR No, you**'re not.**
	Are	you		Yes, I **am.** No, I**'m not.***
	Is	he/she/it		Yes, he/she/it **is.** No, he/she/it **isn't.** OR No, he/she/it**'s not.**
	Are	you		Yes, we **are.** No, we **aren't.** OR No, we**'re not.**
		we		Yes, you **are.** No, you **aren't.** OR No, you**'re not.**
		they		Yes, they **are.** No, they **aren't.** OR No, they**'re not.**

*There is no contraction for *am not*.

3. We do not contract *am*, *is*, and *are* in short answers.

CORRECT: Yes, I am. Yes, she is. Yes, they are.
INCORRECT: Yes, ~~I'm.~~ Yes, ~~she's.~~ Yes, ~~they're.~~

WH– QUESTIONS					
	Wh– Word	*Do/Does*	Subject	Base Verb	
Simple Present	**What**	**do**	I	**need?**	
	Where		you	**live?**	
	Why		we	**study**	so hard?
	When		they	**have**	lunch?
	Who**		you	**like?**	
	Which	**does**	he/she/it	**prefer?**	
	How			**make**	that soup?
	Wh– Word	*Am/Is/Are*	Subject	Verb + *–ing*	
Present Progressive	**Why**	**am**	I	**doing**	your homework?
	Which book		they	**reading?**	
	How	**are**	you	**doing**	that?
	What		we	**working**	on?
	Who**		they	**visiting?**	
	Where	**is**	he/she/it	**going?**	
	When			**leaving?**	

**In formal written English, the wh- word would be *whom*.

The Present Tenses

Complete the conversation with the simple present or the present progressive of the verbs in parentheses. You sometimes need to use short answers.

Woman: Excuse me, (wait) _____are_____ you _____waiting_____ for the flight to London
       1   2
at 10:00?

Man: Yes, I _____.
                    3

Woman: Is this the right gate?

Man: Yes, it is. (live) _____ you _____ in London?
                       4   5

Woman: No, I _____. At the moment, I
                  6
(study) _____ at Cambridge University.
                7

Man: Oh! What (study) _____ you _____?
                    8   9

Woman: I (work) _____ on a degree in business management.
                10

Man: Why (do) _____ you _____ it at Cambridge?
            11   12

Woman: It's a famous university, and my parents (think) _____ it's
                    13
the best. What about you? (go) _____ you often _____ to
                  14   15
London?

Man: Yes, I (go) _____ there on business. I
               16
(have) _____ a meeting there tomorrow.
            17

Woman: Oh. What kind of work (do) _____ you _____?
                  18   19

Man: I (work) _____ for the marketing department of a company.
            20
I often (travel) _____ to different countries around the
            21
world.

Woman: What (do) _____ your company _____?
           22   23

Man: It publishes dictionaries.

Woman: Look! They (board) _____ passengers now. We should
                24
get in line.

20 Practice

Complete the sentences with the simple present or the present progressive of the verb in parentheses.

Kenny Lemkin (work) _____*works*_____ at a bank. He

(go) _____ to work every day. He never

(arrive) _____ late and he rarely (take) _____

a day off. But Kenny (not, be) _____ at work this morning.

Right now, he (pack) _____ a suitcase, and he

(sing) _____. He (look) _____ for his

passport. "Where is it? Oh, I (know) _____ where it is," he thinks.

It's in his pocket. Now Kenny (sit) _____ in a taxi. He

(smile) _____. Now he's on an airplane. It is

(fly) _____ to Rio. Kenny (look) _____

very happy.

21 Practice

Ask and answer these questions about Kenny with a partner.

Example:
Kenny/work/at a restaurant
You: Does Kenny work at a restaurant?
Your partner: No, he doesn't. He works at a bank.

1. Kenny/usually/go/to work every day
2. Kenny/arrive/late
3. Kenny/pack/a suitcase/right now
4. Kenny/look for/his passport
5. Kenny's taxi/go/to the bank
6. Kenny/go/Tokyo

22 What Do You Think?

Do you think Kenny is going on a business trip or on a vacation? Is he going alone? What will he do in Rio?

23 Practice

Read the postcard. Then answer the questions with complete sentences.

Dear Uncle Joe,
    We are on one of the Greek islands. It's called Mykonos. We are staying in a hotel by the beach. We are having a wonderful time. I'm writing this postcard from the hotel. Richard is lying on the beach right now, and Lenny and Linda are swimming in the sea.

    See you soon,
    Laura, Richard, and the kids

Mr. Joseph Kelly
851 W. 37th St.
New York, NY 10006

1. Who is writing the postcard?

   Laura is writing the postcard.

2. Who is she writing to?

   _____

3. Where are Laura and her family staying?

   _____

4. Where is she writing from?

   _____

5. Are they having a good time?

   _____

6. What are Lenny and Linda doing?

   _____

WRITING: Describe a Person

Write a paragraph about your partner.

Step 1. Ask and answer the questions with a partner. Record the answers by checking "Yes" or "No." Write additional information under "Other Information."

	Yes	No	Other Information
1. live/in (city)	_____	_____	_____
2. work	_____	_____	_____
3. like/tennis	_____	_____	_____
4. listen/pop music	_____	_____	_____
5. have/car	_____	_____	_____
6. go/movies on weekends	_____	_____	_____
7. speak/(language)	_____	_____	_____
8. play/the piano	_____	_____	_____
9. go on vacation/in the summer	_____	_____	_____
10. have/brothers and sisters	_____	_____	_____

Step 2. Write sentences about your partner from your notes.

Example:
Kumiko lives in Tokyo.
She doesn't work.
She goes to school.

Step 3. Rewrite the sentences in the form of a paragraph. Write a title (your partner's name). For more writing guidelines, see pages 199–203.

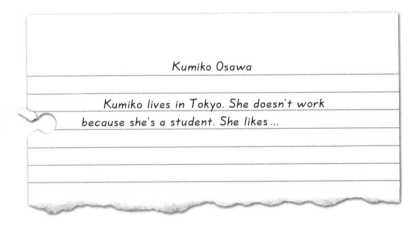

Kumiko Osawa

Kumiko lives in Tokyo. She doesn't work
because she's a student. She likes ...

Step 4. Evaluate your paragraph.

Checklist
_____ Did you indent the first line?
_____ Did you give the paragraph a title?
_____ Did you write the title with a capital letter for each word?

Step 5. Edit your work. Work with a partner or your teacher to edit your sentences. Correct spelling, punctuation, vocabulary, and grammar.

Step 6. Write your final copy.

SELF-TEST

A **Choose the best answer, A, B, C, or D, to complete the sentence. Mark your answer by darkening the oval with the same letter.**

1. Many animals _____ their young in the spring.

   A. are having   Ⓐ Ⓑ Ⓒ Ⓓ
   B. have
   C. has
   D. is have

2. Every year, the Earth _____ around the Sun one time.

   A. travels   Ⓐ Ⓑ Ⓒ Ⓓ
   B. travel
   C. is traveling
   D. does traveling

3. Snow _____ in the Sahara Desert.

   A. sometimes falls   Ⓐ Ⓑ Ⓒ Ⓓ
   B. sometimes is falling
   C. falls sometimes
   D. is falling sometimes

4. Sharks _____ bones.

   A. do not have   Ⓐ Ⓑ Ⓒ Ⓓ
   B. are not having
   C. have not
   D. doesn't have

5. Pandas _____ to eat bamboo.

   A. are preferring   Ⓐ Ⓑ Ⓒ Ⓓ
   B. is preferring
   C. prefer
   D. are prefer

6. At the moment, everybody _____ the football game on television.

   A. is seeing   Ⓐ Ⓑ Ⓒ Ⓓ
   B. is watching
   C. is looking at
   D. does watch

7. We _____ vitamins for good health.

   A. are needing   Ⓐ Ⓑ Ⓒ Ⓓ
   B. need have
   C. have need
   D. need

8. Young children _____ the pictures in books.

   A. always look at   Ⓐ Ⓑ Ⓒ Ⓓ
   B. always see
   C. look at always
   D. always watch

9. When _____ breakfast?

   A. you usually have   Ⓐ Ⓑ Ⓒ Ⓓ
   B. usually have you
   C. do you usually have
   D. you are usually having

10. _____ French?

    A. All Canadians speak   Ⓐ Ⓑ Ⓒ Ⓓ
    B. All Canadians are speaking
    C. Are all Canadians speaking
    D. Do all Canadians speak

B Find the underlined word or phrase, A, B, C, or D, that is incorrect. Mark your answer by darkening the oval with the same letter.

1. Italians <u>usually</u> <u>eats</u> pasta <u>every day</u>
             A   B   C

   <u>of the week</u>.
      D

   Ⓐ Ⓑ Ⓒ Ⓓ

2. <u>How many</u> <u>hours</u> does <u>a baby</u> <u>sleeps</u>?
      A   B   C   D

   Ⓐ Ⓑ Ⓒ Ⓓ

3. <u>People</u> catch <u>sometimes</u> <u>colds</u> <u>in the</u> winter.
      A   B   C   D

   Ⓐ Ⓑ Ⓒ Ⓓ

4. <u>Do</u> bears <u>eat</u> only meat, or <u>they do</u> <u>eat</u>
      A   B   C   D

   plants, too?

   Ⓐ Ⓑ Ⓒ Ⓓ

5. <u>Why</u> <u>are</u> kangaroos only <u>live</u> <u>in Australia</u>?
      A   B   C   D

   Ⓐ Ⓑ Ⓒ Ⓓ

6. In India, the cow <u>gives</u> <u>milk</u> <u>and</u>
                       A   B   C

   <u>is working</u> on the farm.
      D

   Ⓐ Ⓑ Ⓒ Ⓓ

7. Camels <u>do not</u> <u>drink</u> <u>often</u> water for days
             A   B   C

   when they <u>travel</u>.
            D

   Ⓐ Ⓑ Ⓒ Ⓓ

8. When <u>do</u> people <u>use</u> computers, they
          A   B

   <u>often</u> <u>use</u> the Internet to get information.
     C   D

   Ⓐ Ⓑ Ⓒ Ⓓ

9. <u>Men and women</u> in Iceland <u>have</u> long lives
      A   B

   because the air <u>has</u> clean and they <u>have</u>
                 C   D

   good health care.

   Ⓐ Ⓑ Ⓒ Ⓓ

10. People in Thailand <u>not</u> <u>use</u> chopsticks.
                       A   B

    <u>They</u> use <u>spoons</u>.
      C   D

    Ⓐ Ⓑ Ⓒ Ⓓ

UNIT 2

THE PAST TENSES

2a The Simple Past Tense

Pablo Picasso **lived** in France.
He **worked** a lot and **painted** many pictures.

1. To form the simple past tense of regular verbs in affirmative statements, add *–ed* to the base verb.

2. In negative statements, use *did not* + a base verb.

3. In questions, use *did* + a base verb + the subject.

AFFIRMATIVE STATEMENTS		NEGATIVE STATEMENTS		
Subject	Past Tense Verb	Subject	*Did Not/Didn't*	Base Verb
I		I		
You		You		
He/She/It	**worked.**	He/She/It	**did not** **didn't**	**work.**
We		We		
They		They		

YES/NO QUESTIONS			SHORT ANSWERS	
Did	Subject	Base Verb	Yes,	No,
Did	I		you **did.**	you **didn't.**
	you		I/we **did.**	I/we **didn't.**
	he/she/it	**work?**	he/she/it **did.**	he/she/it **didn't.**
	we		you **did.**	you **didn't.**
	they		they **did.**	they **didn't.**

2. We change the spelling of some regular verbs before adding –ed.

Base Verb Ending	Rule	Example	
Most verbs	Add –ed.	start	start**ed**
		obey	obey**ed**
		predict	predict**ed**
The verb ends in a consonant + e.	Add –d.	live	live**d**
		move	move**d**
		decide	decide**d**
The verb ends in a single vowel + a single consonant.	Double the consonant, add –ed.	stop	stop**ped**
		plan	plan**ned**
		prefer	prefer**red**
Exceptions: Do not double w or x.		fix	fix**ed**
		show	show**ed**
If a verb has two or more syllables and the stress is not on the last syllable, do not double the consonant.		open	open**ed**
		travel	travel**ed**
		exit	exit**ed**
		color	color**ed**
The verb ends in a consonant + y.	Change y to i and add –ed.	worry	worr**ied**
		study	stud**ied**
The verb ends in ie.	Add –d.	tie	tie**d**
		die	die**d**

Function

Did Picasso **paint** pictures of his wives?
Yes, he did. He **painted** a lot of them.

We use the simple past tense to talk about actions and situations completed in the past. We often say when the situation or action happened (for example, *yesterday, last night*).

1 | Practice

Write the -ed forms of the verbs.

Base Verb	-ed Form
1. listen	_listened_
2. wait	_____
3. study	_____
4. die	_____
5. stay	_____
6. admit	_____
7. rain	_____
8. start	_____
9. happen	_____
10. tie	_____
11. open	_____
12. hope	_____

2 | Practice

Complete the sentences. Use the simple past tense of the verbs in parentheses.

Pablo Picasso was born in Malaga, Spain in 1881. His first word was "lápiz"

(Spanish for pencil), and he (learn) _____learned_____ to draw before he
                                        1

(talk) _____. He (hate) _____ school. He
            2   3

(like) _____ to paint pictures instead. His father was an artist.
            4

Pablo often (watch) _____ him paint pictures. One day, he
                          5

(finish) _____ one of his father's paintings. When his father
              6

(return) _____, he (not, believe) _____ it. It was
              7   8

wonderful! His father never (paint) _____ again. Pablo was only 13.
                                          9

    Picasso (travel) _____ to Paris. He (live) _____ in
                          10   11

a small room. He sometimes (work) _____ by the light of a candle. Many
                                        12

people (realize) _____ that he was a genius.
                      13

    One day, a French minister (visit) _____ Picasso. Some paint
                                              14

(spill) _____ on the minister's trousers by accident. Picasso
              15

(apologize) _____ and (want) _____ to pay to clean
                16   17
them. The minister said, "No, please, Monsieur Picasso, just sign my trousers." His

paintings (change) _____ people's ideas about art. Picasso
                        18
(love) _____ to paint. He (not, stop) _____. He
            19   20
(continue) _____ to paint until the end. He (die) _____
                21   22
at the age of 91.

3 | Practice

Write a question using the prompts. Then write a negative statement. Finally, write a correct sentence using words from the list.

France	Paris	the United States
Juliet	radium	Thomas Edison
Mount Everest	slower	

1. Pablo Picasso/live/in London

   Did Pablo Picasso live in London?

   No, he didn't live in London.

   He lived in Paris.

2. Charlie Chaplin/invent/the light bulb

   _____

   _____

   _____

3. Marie and Pierre Curie/discover/penicillin

   _____

   _____

   _____

4. Marilyn Monroe/come/from France

   _____

   _____

   _____

5. engineers/construct/the Statue of Liberty/in the United States

   _____

   _____

   _____

6. trains/travel/faster/50 years ago

_____

_____

_____

7. Romeo/love/Cleopatra

_____

_____

_____

8. Sir Edmund Hillary and Tenzing Norgay/climb/Mount Fuji

_____

_____

_____

2b Irregular Verbs

Marie Curie **was** a famous scientist.
Marie **went** to Paris to study.
There, she **met** Pierre Curie.

Many common verbs do not end in _–ed_ for the simple past. They are irregular. Here is the past form of the verb _go_.

AFFIRMATIVE STATEMENTS		NEGATIVE STATEMENTS		
Subject	Past Tense Verb	Subject	_Did Not/Didn't_	Base Verb
I		I		
You		You		
He/She/It	**went** to Paris.	He/She/It	**did not** **didn't**	**go** to Paris.
We		We		
They		They		

YES/NO QUESTIONS			SHORT ANSWERS	
Did	Subject	Base Verb	Yes,	No,
Did	I		you **did.**	you **didn't.**
	you		I/we **did.**	I/we **didn't.**
	he/she/it	**go** to Paris?	he/she/it **did.**	he/she/it **didn't.**
	we		you **did.**	you **didn't.**
	they		they **did.**	they **didn't.**

WH– QUESTIONS			
Wh– Word	*Did*	Subject	Base Verb
When		I	**go** to Tokyo?
Where		you	**go** last night?
Why	**did**	he/she/it	**go** out?
Who*		we	**go** out with last week?
How (often)		they	**go** out last week?

*In formal written English, the wh- word would be *whom*.
See page 196 for a list of irregular verbs.

4 | Practice

Complete the sentences with the simple past tense of the verbs in parentheses. Use the list of irregular verbs on page 196.

Maria Sklodowska was born in Poland. She (have) _____*had*_____ a sister,
                                                            1
Bronya. Maria was a good student. She (love) _____ science. She and her
                                                            2
sister (want) _____ to go to college. In those days, women
                    3
(not, go) _____ to college in Poland. So Maria and Bronya
              4
(decide) _____ to go to Paris to study. It was expensive for two girls to
              5
study at one time. Bronya (leave) _____ for Paris first. Maria
                                            6
(work) _____ as a teacher in Poland. She (send) _____
            7   8
money to Bronya. Bronya (finish) _____ her studies, and then she
                                            9
(help) _____ Maria to study.
            10
    Maria (become) _____ a student at the Sorbonne University
                          11
in Paris. In Paris, she (change) _____ her name to Marie. She
                                      12
(study) _____ science. She (not, have) _____ much money.
            13   14

She (live) _____ in a small room. She (climb) _____ six
                    15   16
floors to her room. It (not, have) _____ any electricity or water. She
                                              17
(eat) _____ very little.
              18
   One day, she (meet) _____ Pierre Curie, and her life
                                  19
(change) _____. They (marry) _____ one year later.
                20   21
Pierre was also a scientist. They (work) _____ together a lot. Together they
                                                        22
(discover) _____ radium. They (win) _____ a Nobel Prize
                    23   24
for the discovery. Three years later, Pierre (die) _____ in an accident.
                                                                25
Marie was very sad, but she (continue) _____ her work. In 1911, she
                                                    26
(get) _____ another Nobel Prize. Marie (give) _____
              27   28
her life to her work. She (die) _____ in 1934 from cancer.
                                          29
   Marie (have) _____ a daughter, Irene. Irene
                          30
(continue) _____ her mother's work. She, too,
                    31
(receive) _____ a Nobel Prize. Irene died of cancer, too.
                  32

5 Practice

Write questions with the prompts and then answer them with short answers.

1. Marie/study in Poland

   Did Marie study in Poland?

   No, she didn't.

2. women/go to college in Poland

   _____

   _____

3. Marie/send her sister money from Poland

   _____

   _____

4. Marie/study at the university in Paris

   _____

   _____

5. Marie/have a lot of money

   _____

   _____

6. Marie/meet Pierre in Paris

_____

_____

7. Marie and Pierre/marry

_____

_____

8. Marie and Pierre Curie/win the Nobel Prize

_____

_____

9. Pierre/die in an accident

_____

_____

10. Marie/have a son

_____

_____

11. Irene/become an actress

_____

_____

12. Irene/receive a Nobel Prize

_____

_____

6 | Your Turn

Tell your classmates or your partner about your life. Use the simple past tense.

Example:
I was born in Peru. When I was two, we went to live in Mexico City.

7 | Practice

Complete the paragraphs with the simple past tense of the verbs in parentheses.

A.

Elvis Presley was born in 1935 in Mississippi. He (spend) _____*spent*_____ a lot

              1

of time with African-American musicians. He (learn) _____ a lot from them.

              2

In 1953, he (pay) _____ to make a record for his mother's birthday. The

              3

owner of the record company (listen) _____ to it and

(like) _____ it. Then, he (offer) _____ Elvis work.

His first record, in 1954, was a hit. Teenagers (love) _____ it. They

(scream) _____ when they saw Elvis. Elvis (record) _____

94 gold singles. He (star) _____ in 27 films. Elvis continued to be

famous, and he (perform) _____ in many concerts. His life

(end) _____ sadly. He (die) _____ at the age of 42. Radio

stations (play) _____ his songs, and his fans (cry) _____.

B.

James Dean was born in 1931. His mother (die) _____ when he was

young. He (live) _____ with his uncle and aunt on their farm. Later, he

(study) _____ acting for two years. Then he (start) _____

to work in theater and the movies. He also (appear) _____ in a TV

commercial. In 1954, he (act) _____ in a play. Some important people from

Hollywood (like) _____ him in the play. They (offer) _____

him a movie contract. James Dean (star) _____ in only three films, but

he (become) _____ popular. He (die) _____ in a car crash

in 1955.

2c   The Past Progressive Tense

Form

We **were playing** outside.
The sky **was getting** darker.
Then we saw it. A tornado!
It **was coming** this way!

1. We form the past progressive tense with a past form of *be* (*was* or *were*) and verb + *–ing*.

2. See page 198 for spelling rules for *–ing* verb forms.

AFFIRMATIVE AND NEGATIVE STATEMENTS

Subject	*Was/Were (Not)*	Verb + *–ing*
I	was was not wasn't	working.
You	were were not weren't	
He/She/It	was was not wasn't	
We	were were not weren't	
They	were were not weren't	

YES/NO QUESTIONS			SHORT ANSWERS	
Was/Were	Subject	Verb + *–ing*	Yes,	No,
Was	I	**working?**	you **were.**	you **weren't.**
Were	you		I **was.**	I **wasn't.**
Was	he/she/it		he/she/it **was.**	he/she/it **wasn't.**
Were	we		you **were.**	you **weren't.**
	you		we **were.**	we **weren't.**
	they		they **were.**	they **weren't.**

WH– QUESTIONS

Wh– Word	*Was/Were*	Subject	Verb + *–ing*
How (fast)	**was**	the tornado	**moving?**
What		I	**saying?**
Who*		she	**calling?**
Where	**were**	you	**going** yesterday?
Why		they	**studying** at midnight?
Why		they	**sleeping** in class?

*In formal written English, the wh– word would be *whom*.

We use the past progressive tense to describe an action in progress at a particular time in the past.

We were watching the news on television at 6:00 last night.

8 Practice

Complete the sentences with the past progressive tense of the verbs in parentheses.

1. Last night, television and radio stations (warn) ___*were warning*___ people about the tornado.

2. It (get) _____ closer.

3. People (run) _____ for shelter.

4. The tornado (destroy) _____ everything in its way.

5. We (not, watch) _____ television.

6. We (study) _____ in the library.

7. Suddenly the librarian started shouting. She (tell) _____ us to run to the basement.

9 Practice

Complete the sentences with the past progressive of the verbs in parentheses.

Amanda Ferguson (drive) _____*was driving*_____ to her mother's house. She
                                                    1
(not, listen) _____ to the radio. She didn't know that a tornado
                          2
(come) _____ toward her.
                3
   The sky (get) _____ darker and darker, but she thought
                              4
it was just an ordinary storm. Suddenly, there was a big noise. It was as dark as

night, and the wind (blow) _____ very hard. Pieces of houses
                                        5
and trees (fly) _____ everywhere. Then she knew what
                        6
(happen) _____. She was inside a tornado!
              7
   Amanda screamed. Then she saw her mother's house. But she

(look) _____ down at it from 25 feet in the air! Amanda was
              8
lucky! The tornado dropped the car in her mother's back yard. She lived to tell the story.

10 | Practice

Read the paragraph. Then write wh- questions for the answers. Use the wh- word in parentheses and the past progressive tense.

> Susan was walking on the beach. She noticed that the wind was blowing very hard. The waves were crashing on the sand. Black clouds were coming toward the land very fast. When she got back to the house, her husband was covering the windows with wood. A hurricane was coming!

1. (where) _Where was Susan walking?_____

   Answer: She was walking on the beach.

2. (how hard) _____

   Answer: It was blowing very hard.

3. (where) _____

   Answer: On the sand.

4. (how fast) _____

   Answer: They were coming very fast.

5. (when) _____

   Answer: When she got home.

11 | Your Turn

Say four things that were happening last night at 8:00.

Example:
I was sitting on the sofa in my apartment. My brother was watching television.

2d The Simple Past Tense OR The Past Progressive Tense

Ken Johnson **was riding** his bicycle when a tornado **lifted** him into the air. While he **was flying** through the sky, he **saw** a horse right next to him! The boy **was crying** when the tornado **put** him down safely in a field.

1. We often use the past progressive and simple past tenses together in a sentence. The past progressive describes the longer action that was in progress in the past; the simple past describes the shorter action that happened in the middle of the longer action.

   I **was working** when I **heard** the tornado.

2. We use the simple past, not the past progressive, to show that one action followed another.

   I **picked up** my baby when I **heard** the tornado.
   (First she heard the tornado. Then she picked up her baby.)

3. When one action interrupts another, we use *when* before the simple past action or *while* before the past progressive action.

   I was hiding in the basement **when** the tornado passed over my house.
   While I was hiding in the basement, the tornado passed over my house.

4. We can change the order of the parts of a sentence with *when* or *while*.

   When the tornado passed over my house, I was hiding in the basement.
   The tornado passed over my house **while** I was hiding in the basement.

   When we begin a sentence with *when* or *while* plus a subject and a verb, we put a comma between the two parts.

5. We use the past progressive with two actions that continued at the same time in the past. We use *while* to show the actions were happening at the same time.

   While I was hiding in the basement, my husband was looking for me.

6. Remember, we do not usually use the present progressive tense with nonprogressive verbs. (See page 15.) The same is true for the past progressive tense.

   CORRECT: We saw the tornado.
   INCORRECT: We ~~were seeing~~ the tornado.

---

12 Practice

Complete the sentences with the simple past or past progressive of the verbs in parentheses.

It (rain) _____*was raining*_____ very hard when the bus
$_1$

(leave) _____ the school. When we
$_2$

(get) _____ home, my Aunt Millie and Uncle Ben
$_3$

(wait) _____ for us. They (tell) _____
$_4$ $_5$

us to run into their storm cellar underground. When I (look) _____
$_6$

up the road, I (see) _____ that a tornado (come)
$_7$

_____ toward our house. We all (run) _____
$_8$ $_9$

toward the shelter. But it was too late. The tornado (pass) _____
$_{10}$

over us while we (try) _____ to get down the stairs.
$_{11}$

We (close) _____ the door when the wind suddenly
$_{12}$

(pull) _____ it off. The noise was as loud as a train, and
$_{13}$

it was very dark. My uncle (hold) _____ me down when suddenly
$_{14}$

the tornado (lift) _____ him and threw him against a wall.
$_{15}$

Everyone (scream) _____ for help while the tornado
$_{16}$

(throw) _____ things on top of us. Suddenly the wind
$_{17}$

(stop) _____. It (become) _____ very
$_{18}$ $_{19}$

quiet. My uncle and sister were hurt, but we all (survive) _____.
$_{20}$

13 Your Turn

One of your classmates did not come to school yesterday. He/she had a cold.
Imagine what he/she was doing while you were studying at school.

Example:
While we were doing exercises in our English class, my classmate was resting in bed.

2e   Past Time Clauses

Form / Function

When young Mozart played,
everyone listened.

1. A clause is a group of words with a subject and a verb. Some clauses are main
   clauses. A main clause can stand alone as a complete sentence. This sentence is a
   main clause.

   Mozart played for the queen.

2. Time clauses start with words like *when, while, before,* or *after.* Time clauses are
   dependent clauses. We must use dependent clauses with a main clause.

Main Clause	Time Clause
Everyone listened	**when he played.**

3. We can put a time clause at the beginning or the end of a sentence. If the time clause comes first, we use a comma after it.

> **While he was speaking,** he stood up.
> He stood up **while he was speaking.**

> **Before he took the money,** he counted it.
> He counted the money **before he took it.**

4. In a sentence with a clause starting with *when,* both verbs can be in the simple past tense.

> **When** they **asked,** he **sang.**
> (First they asked. Then he sang.)

14 Practice

Complete the sentences with the correct form of the verbs in parentheses.

Mozart was born in Austria in 1756. When he (be) _____*was*_____
1

four years old, he (start) _____ to play the piano. His father
2

(teach) _____ him. Before he (be) _____
3   4

five, he (begin) _____ to write music. When he
5

(be) _____ six, he (give) _____ concerts all
6   7

over Europe. He (play) _____ for important people like kings and
8

queens. They (pay) _____ a lot of money to hear him. Mozart's
9

family (need) _____ the money to live. Once, he
10

(go) _____ to Vienna and (play) _____
11   12

for the Empress Maria Theresa. She (love) _____ Mozart's playing.
13

When he (finish) _____, he (climb) _____
14   15

up on her knee and (give) _____ her a kiss.
16

When he (be) _____ 11, he
17

(write) _____ an opera. One time, when
18

he (be) _____ 14 years old, he
19

(hear) _____ music in the Sistine Chapel in Rome. When
20

he (get) _____ home, he (remember) _____
                 21   22
everything and (write) _____ it down exactly.
                              23

   Mozart (marry) _____ Constanze Weber. They
                          24

(be) _____ happy together and (have) _____
              25   26
six children. Mozart (work) _____ hard because he always
                                      27

(have) _____ money problems. He
                28

(begin) _____ to work in the evening and often
                 29

(work) _____ all night. He (like) _____
                30   31
to write while he (stand) _____ up. He
                                 32

(sleep) _____ very little. Mozart (die) _____
                 33   34
at the age of 35. No one (go) _____ to his funeral.
                                     35

 Your Turn

Say four things you did after you went home yesterday.

Example:
After I went home yesterday, I changed my clothes.

2f *Used To*

Form

Three hundred years ago, life in North America was very different. People **used to carry** lanterns for light. They **didn't use to have** electricity.

Used to + base verb takes the same form in all persons.

AFFIRMATIVE STATEMENTS		NEGATIVE STATEMENTS	
Subject	*Used To* + Base Verb	Subject	*Didn't Use To* + Base Verb
I		I	
You		You	
He/She/It	**used to work** hard.	He/She/It	**didn't use to work** hard.
We		We	
They		They	

YES/NO QUESTIONS			SHORT ANSWERS	
Did	Subject	*Use To* + Base Verb	Yes,	No,
	I		you **did.**	you **didn't.**
	you		I/we **did.**	I/we **didn't.**
Did	he/she/it	**use to work** hard?	he/she/it **did.**	he/she/it **didn't.**
	we		you **did.**	you **didn't.**
	they		they **did.**	they **didn't.**

Function

We use *used to* when we want to emphasize the fact that a habit or situation no longer exists.

Most people **used to walk** or ride horses. Today they drive cars.
They **used to wash** clothes by hand. Today they have washing machines.
They **didn't use to drink** water because it often wasn't clean. Today people can drink water because it is clean.

16 Practice

Rewrite the sentences using *used to* or *did/didn't use to*.

1. Did people wash a lot?

   Did people use to wash a lot?

2. No, people didn't wash very often.

   No, people didn't use to wash very often.

3. Why didn't they wash often?

   Why didn't they use to wash often?

4. They didn't have water inside the house.

   _____

5. Did people live for a long time?

_____

6. No, most people lived a short life.

_____

7. They didn't have many doctors.

_____

8. A doctor visited a town a few times a year.

_____

9. Mothers made medicines for the family from plants.

_____

10. Most of the medicines tasted bad.

_____

11. Some of these medicines killed people.

_____

17 Practice

Rewrite the sentences using _used to_ or _did/didn't use to_.

Life was very different in the early English colonies in North America from the way it is today.

1. How did people eat?

How did people use to eat?

2. Did people eat with their fingers?

_____

3. Yes, they did. It was good manners to eat with your fingers.

_____

4. In many homes, there was one big pot on the table.

_____

5. People put their fingers into the pot to take out food.

_____

6. People didn't have plates.

_____

7. They used a wooden board.

_____

8. Did children eat with the father and mother?

_____

9. Yes, they did. But children didn't talk at the table. They didn't even sit down.

_____

_____

10. Did they stand up through the whole meal?

_____

11. Yes, children stood up through the whole meal.

_____

12. What did people do when they had a toothache?

_____

13. People went to the barber when they had a toothache. Barbers pulled teeth.

_____

_____

14. What furniture did they have then?

_____

15. They didn't have much furniture in the 1600s.

_____

16. Many families had only one chair.

_____

17. Where did the father sit?

_____

18. The father always sat in the chair.

_____

[18] Practice

Find and correct the errors in the underlined parts of the sentences. Some sentences have no errors. Tommy's grandparents live on a farm far away. He is going to visit them for the first time. He is asking his mother questions.

Tommy: How do they cook their food? Do they use wood?

                used to burn
Mother: No. They ~~used burn~~ wood in the stove, but now they have electricity.
                1

Tommy: <u>Did they used to buy</u> their wood?
          2

Mother: No, they didn't. They <u>used to cut</u> it themselves.
                                3

Tommy: <u>Used they to grow</u> their own food?
          4

Mother: Yes, they did. They <u>use to grow</u> almost everything. But now they buy many
                               5
          things at the store.

Tommy: Where do they get their water?

Mother: Well, they <u>use get</u> it from a stream, but now they have a well.
                      6

Tommy: Do they have lots of animals?

Mother: Only a few. They <u>used to have</u> lots of animals.
                            7

Tommy: <u>What animals used they have?</u>
                        8

Mother: They <u>use to have</u> lots of chickens, cows, and goats.
               9

Tommy: What <u>did you used do</u> for fun when you were little?
               10

Mother: Oh, we <u>used to sing,</u> play games, read, and listen to the radio.
                  11

Tommy: Will I be able to watch television?

Mother: Of course. They <u>didn't used to have</u> television, but they do now.
                           12

Your Turn

A. Write four things you used to do as a child that you do not do now.

Example:
When I was a child, I used to cry a lot. Now I don't.

1. _____

2. _____

3. _____

4. _____

B. Share your sentences with a partner. Then write four things that your partner said.

Example:
When she was a child, she used to climb trees.

1. _____

2. _____

3. _____

4. _____

WRITING: Describe a Time in the Past

Write a description of life in your country 100 years ago.

Step 1. Work with a partner. Ask and answer questions about life 100 years ago. The prompts below will help you, or you can use your own ideas.

Example:
go out at night a lot
You: Did people use to go out at night a lot?
Your partner: No, they didn't. They sometimes used to go to concerts or the theater.

1. go out at night a lot

2. cook on a stove that burns wood

3. go to the movies together

4. eat at home

5. watch television

6. listen to the radio

7. read magazines

8. play games at home

9. wear different clothes

Step 2. Write the answers to the questions. Then rewrite the answers in paragraph form. Write a title in a few words (Life One Hundred Years Ago). For more writing guidelines, see pages 199–203.

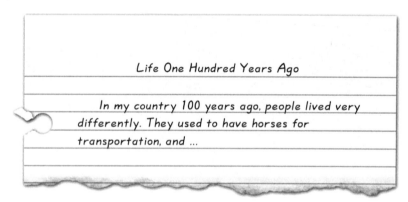

Life One Hundred Years Ago

In my country 100 years ago, people lived very differently. They used to have horses for transportation, and ...

Step 3. Evaluate your paragraph.

Checklist

_____ Did you indent the first line?

_____ Did you give your paragraph a title?

_____ Did you put the title in the center of the page?

Step 4. Edit your work. Work with your partner or your teacher to edit your sentences. Correct spelling, punctuation, vocabulary, and grammar.

Step 5. Write your final copy.

SELF-TEST

A   Choose the best answer, A, B, C, or D, to complete the sentence. Mark your answer by darkening the oval with the same letter.

1. Ken _____ in a rock group, but now he doesn't.

   A. sang   Ⓐ Ⓑ Ⓒ Ⓓ
   B. sung
   C. used to sing
   D. was singing

2. When the earthquake struck, people _____.

   A. slept   Ⓐ Ⓑ Ⓒ Ⓓ
   B. used to sleep
   C. are sleeping
   D. were sleeping

3. Alexander Graham Bell _____ the telephone in 1876.

   A. invent   Ⓐ Ⓑ Ⓒ Ⓓ
   B. invented
   C. used to invent
   D. were inventing

4. It _____ while people were waiting for the bus.

   A. is raining   Ⓐ Ⓑ Ⓒ Ⓓ
   B. rains
   C. used to rain
   D. was raining

5. Early colonists _____ to wash a lot.

   A. did not use   Ⓐ Ⓑ Ⓒ Ⓓ
   B. did not used
   C. used not
   D. did use not

6. Why _____ young?

   A. people died   Ⓐ Ⓑ Ⓒ Ⓓ
   B. died people
   C. did people die
   D. people did die

7. _____ have doctors in 1800?

   A. Used they to   Ⓐ Ⓑ Ⓒ Ⓓ
   B. Did they use to
   C. Did they used to
   D. Did use to they

8. The students were taking the test when they _____ the noise.

   A. were hearing   Ⓐ Ⓑ Ⓒ Ⓓ
   B. were heard
   C. hear
   D. heard

9. What _____ last night?

   A. you did   Ⓐ Ⓑ Ⓒ Ⓓ
   B. you did do
   C. did you do
   D. you do

10. While the spectators _____ the game, part of the stadium collapsed.

   A. were watching   Ⓐ Ⓑ Ⓒ Ⓓ
   B. watching
   C. watched
   D. was watching

B **Find the underlined word or phrase, A, B, C, or D, that is incorrect. Mark your answer by darkening the oval with the same letter.**

1. <u>When</u> Van Gogh <u>moved</u> from Holland <u>to</u>
     A   B   C
   France, he <u>start</u> to paint with bright colors.
           D

   Ⓐ Ⓑ Ⓒ Ⓓ

2. <u>While</u> Marie <u>studying</u> <u>at</u> the university,
     A   B   C
   she <u>married</u> Pierre Curie.
       D

   Ⓐ Ⓑ Ⓒ Ⓓ

3. Harriet Beecher Stowe <u>worked</u> on her
                        A
   book <u>after</u> everyone <u>was going</u> <u>to bed</u>.
       B   C   D

   Ⓐ Ⓑ Ⓒ Ⓓ

4. Charles Lindberg <u>flown</u> alone <u>across</u> <u>the</u>
                 A   B   C
   Atlantic Ocean <u>in 1927</u>.
            D

   Ⓐ Ⓑ Ⓒ Ⓓ

5. Louis Braille <u>invented</u> a system of writing
            A
   <u>for</u> blind people <u>when</u> he <u>was teaching</u> in
    B   C   D
   a school for them.

   Ⓐ Ⓑ Ⓒ Ⓓ

6. <u>When</u> Franklin D. Roosevelt <u>become</u>
     A   B
   president, <u>the United States</u> <u>was suffering</u>
              C   D
   from hard times.

   Ⓐ Ⓑ Ⓒ Ⓓ

7. <u>When</u> the Englishman Scott <u>reached</u> the
     A   B
   South Pole, he <u>seen</u> the <u>Norwegian flag</u>.
               C   D

   Ⓐ Ⓑ Ⓒ Ⓓ

8. <u>When</u> the German immigrants <u>arrived</u> in
     A   B
   the United States in the 1800s, <u>they</u>
                           C
   <u>were bringing</u> the hamburger steak
      D
   with them.

   Ⓐ Ⓑ Ⓒ Ⓓ

9. <u>While</u> he <u>was hiking</u> in the Alps,
     A   B
   Georges de Mestral <u>was getting</u> the idea
                     C
   for <u>Velcro</u>®.
       D

   Ⓐ Ⓑ Ⓒ Ⓓ

10. In ancient Rome, a wife <u>use to wear</u> <u>her</u>
                          A   B
    gold ring in public, but <u>at home</u> she <u>wore</u>
                      C   D
    a ring made of iron.

    Ⓐ Ⓑ Ⓒ Ⓓ

UNIT 3

THE FUTURE TENSES

3a Be Going To

The astronauts are in the spacecraft. The engines are making a loud noise. Everyone is counting 10, 9, 8, 7. In a few seconds, the spacecraft **is going to take off.** It **is going to travel** in space for 30 days. The astronauts **are not going to visit** other planets.

AFFIRMATIVE AND NEGATIVE STATEMENTS, FULL FORMS, AND CONTRACTIONS

Subject	Am/Is/Are (Not)	Going To	Base Verb
I	**am** **'m** **am not** **'m not**		
You	**are** **'re** **are not** **'re not** **aren't**		
He/She/It	**is** **'s** **is not** **'s not** **isn't**	**going to**	**leave.**
We	**are** **'re**		
They	**are not** **'re not** **aren't**		

YES/NO QUESTIONS				SHORT ANSWERS	
Am/Is/Are	Subject	*Going To*	Base Verb	Yes,	No,
Am	I			you **are.**	you**'re not.** / you **aren't.**
Are	you			I **am.**	I**'m not.**
Is	he/she/it	**going to**	**leave?**	he/she/it **is.**	he/she/it**'s not.** / he/she/it **isn't.**
	we			you **are.**	you**'re not.** / you **aren't.**
Are	you			we **are.**	we**'re not.** / we **aren't.**
	they			they **are.**	they**'re not.** / they **aren't.**

Note: We often pronounce *going to* as "gonna."

Function

1. We use *be going to* + a base verb to talk about plans for the future.

   The astronaut **is going to do** some experiments in space.
   The spacecraft **is going to travel** in space for 30 days.

2. We use *be going to* + a base verb to talk about something in the future that we can see as a result of something in the present.

   The engines are making a loud noise. In a few seconds, the spacecraft **is going to take** off.

   Be careful! You**'re going to fall!**

1 Practice

Complete the sentences with the *be going to* form of the verb in parentheses.

In a minute, the astronauts (enter) _____are going to enter_____
                                              1

the spacecraft. The air in the spacecraft is different. The astronauts

(not, have) _____ any weight. They
                        2

(do) _____ everyday things in a different way.
              3

They (not, sleep) _____ in regular beds. They
                              4

(sleep) _____ in hanging beds. They
                  5

(fold) _____ their arms when they sleep. This holds their
                    6

arms in place. It (be) _____ difficult to take a shower.
                                    7

It (take) _____ a long time because they need special
                    8

equipment.

2 Practice

What is going to happen in these situations on a spacecraft? Write a question and a negative answer with *be going to*. Use the prompts in parentheses.

1. One astronaut misses her family. She picks up a special phone.

   (call, her boss) *Is she going to call her boss?*

   No, she is going to call her family.

2. Today's astronauts have free time. Astronaut Robert Barnes has some music on CDs with him.

   (listen, to a baseball game) _____

   _____

3. Astronaut Nadia Smith likes to look at the Earth from the window. She has some free time in half an hour.

   (watch, television) _____

   _____

4. It's time for lunch. The astronauts have special trays in front of them like airplane food.

   (eat, breakfast) _____

   _____

5. Robert is putting on a special suit. He plans to take a walk in space.

   (take a walk, inside the station) _____

   _____

6. Nadia feels tired. She didn't sleep well.

   (rest, tomorrow) _____

   _____

3 Your Turn

Tell your partner five things you are going to do when you go home today. Then tell the class what your partner is going to do.

Example:
I'm going to relax, and then I'm going to do my homework.

3b *Will*

Form

Scientists want to build colonies in space in the future. The first colony **will be** 240,000 miles from Earth. Thousands of people **will live** and **work** in the colony.

AFFIRMATIVE AND NEGATIVE STATEMENTS

Subject	Will (Not)	Base Verb
I	**will**	
You	**'ll**	
He/She/It		**leave.**
We	**will not**	
They	**won't**	

YES/NO QUESTIONS — SHORT ANSWERS

Will	Subject	Base Verb	Yes,	No,
	I		you **will.**	you **won't.**
	you		I/we **will.**	I/we **won't.**
Will	he/she/it	**leave?**	he/she/it **will.**	he/she/it **won't.**
	we		you **will.**	you **won't.**
	they		they **will.**	they **won't.**

Function

1. We use *will* + a base verb to make predictions about the future or what we think will happen.

   People **will live** in space colonies.
   There **won't be** any pollution in space colonies.

2. We use *will* when we decide to do something at the moment of speaking.

> A: We need some help here.
> B: OK. I**'ll be** there in 10 minutes.

> A: Which one do you want? The red one or the blue one?
> B: I**'ll take** the red one.

3. We often use *probably* with *will*. *Probably* usually comes between *will* and the base verb.

> I**'ll probably see** you tomorrow.
> Olga **will probably call** us tonight.
> She**'ll probably not call** us tomorrow.
> OR She **probably won't call** us tomorrow.

4. We can use verbs like *intend, hope,* and *plan* to express future events and situations. Use the simple present tense followed by an infinitive (*to* + base verb).

> They **plan** (now) **to build** a colony in space (in the future).

4 Practice

Complete the sentences with *will* or the simple present of the verbs in parentheses.

1. Space colonies (be) _____*will be*_____ islands in space.

2. They (not, be) _____ on planets. They (be) _____ in space.

3. A space colony (not, have) _____ bad weather.

4. The people (control) _____ the weather in the colony.

5. A space colony (look) _____ like a wheel in space.

6. Scientists (intend) _____ to have more than 10,000 people on the colony.

7. They (plan) _____ to have animals on the colony.

8. The colony (not, need) _____ gasoline.

9. Cars (run) _____ on electricity.

10. Scientists think it (take) _____ 25 years to build a space colony.

11. It (cost) _____ hundreds of billions of dollars.

12. They (hope) _____ to build the colony in this century.

5 Practice

Andy is 16 years old now. What will he be like 10 years from now? Use the prompts and *will* or *won't* to write sentences that Andy could say about himself.

1. I/probably/have a job

   I'll probably have a job.

2. I/be married

   _____

3. I/probably/have children

   _____

4. I/not/be/a millionaire

   _____

5. I/not/look the same as I do now

   _____

6. I/probably/have a nice car

   _____

7. I/probably/live in an apartment

   _____

8. I/probably/not/live in the city

   _____

Say which of the sentences in Practice 5 will be true for you.

Example:
I will probably have a job.

What do you intend to do tonight? What do you hope to do next week? What do you plan to do next summer?

Example:
I intend to call my family tonight.

3c *Be Going To* OR *Will*

Function

"I'**ll take** 10 oranges, please."

"Look! It'**s going to rain.**"

Will	Be Going To
1. We use *will* for actions that we decide at the moment of speaking. A: The tomato sauce splashed all over my shirt. B: Don't worry. I'**ll clean** it for you.	1. We use *be going to* for actions that we have already decided to do. A: Why are you moving the furniture? B: I'**m going to clean** the floor.
2. We use *will* to talk about things that we think or believe will happen in the future. A: It's time for the news on television. B: Let's watch it. I think it **will be** interesting.	2. We use *be going to* to talk about something in the future that will be a result of something in the present. A: I want to watch the news. I'**m going to turn** on the television.

Practice

Complete the sentences with *be going to* or *will* and the verbs in parentheses.

A.

A: My father is coming to dinner tonight, so I (make) __*am going to make*__ a
   1
   special dessert. Oh no! I don't have any sugar. Can you go to the store for me?

B: Sure, I (go) _____.
   2

A: Take an umbrella with you. Look at the sky! It (rain) _____.
   3

B: This umbrella is broken. I (take) _____ your umbrella, OK?
   4

B.

A: I (go) _____ to the new mall tomorrow.
   1

B: Oh, what (get) _____ you _____?
   2   3

A: I (look) _____ for a pair of brown shoes.
   4

B: I'm free tomorrow. I (go) _____ with you.
   5

C.

A: We (have) _____ a meeting at 5:00 tomorrow.
   1

B: OK. I (see) _____ you there.
   2

D.

A: What (do) _____ you _____ for your vacation this summer?
   1   2

B: I don't know. I (probably, spend) _____ my vacation with
   3
   my parents. They (rent) _____ a small house by the beach
   4
   for a month.

E.

A: I (leave) _____ at 4:30. The traffic is really bad on Friday
   1
   evenings.

B: You're right. I think I (do) _____ the same.
   2

9

Practice

Complete the sentences with *will* or *be going to* and the verbs in parentheses.

1. Thanks for lending me this book. I (give) _____ `ll give _____ it back to you
   when I see you again.

2. A: I have a terrible headache.

   B: Wait. I (get) _____ an aspirin for you.

3. Don't make so much noise. You (wake) _____ everybody up.

4. This plant is not growing. It does not look good. I think it (die)

   _____.

5. This food looks terrible. I (not, eat) _____ it.

6. Look at that smoke! That battery (blow up) _____!

7. Don't worry about the mess. I (clean) _____ it up.

3d The Present Progressive Tense to Express Future Time

Function

John is in a hurry. He**'s giving** a
presentation to his boss in fifteen minutes,
and at 12:00 he**'s leaving** for Texas.

We can use the present progressive to talk about future plans.

10 | Practice

Look at Janet's schedule for next week. Then use the present progressive tense to complete the sentences about her plans.

Schedule

Monday:	Have lunch with John at 1:00. Go to gym after work.
Tuesday:	Attend meetings from 8:00 to 4:00.
Wednesday:	Go to the doctor at 1:30.
Thursday:	Pick up photos at 6:00.
Friday:	Meet Pamela outside the movie theater at 7:00.
Saturday:	Go to Ken and Stella's house for dinner at 7:30.
Sunday:	Play tennis with Mary at 10:00.

1. _She's having lunch with John_ _____ at 1:00.

2. _____ after work on Monday.

3. _____ from 8:00 to 4:00 on Tuesday.

4. _____ at 1:30 on Wednesday.

5. _____ at 6:00 on Thursday.

6. _____ outside the movie theater at 7:00 on Friday.

7. _____ for dinner at 7:30 on Saturday.

8. _____ at 10:00 on Sunday.

Look at Jim's schedule for tomorrow. Then complete the conversation about his plans with the present progressive of the verbs in parentheses.

Schedule

8:00	Leave the house for the airport
9:30	Catch the plane to San Francisco
12:00	Have lunch with Carlos at the Blue Moon Restaurant
2:00	Go to the San Francisco office and work until 5:00
6:00	Meet Judy in the office lobby
6:30	Have dinner with Judy and Dave at the Prado restaurant
9:30	Catch the plane back home

Ken: What (do) ____are____ you _____doing_____ tomorrow Jim?
　　　　　　　　　　1　　　　　　　　　　　　　2

Jim: I (go) _____ to San Francisco.
　　　　　　　　　　3

Ken: What time (leave) _____ you _____?
　　　　　　　　　　　　　4　　　　　　　　5

Jim: I (leave) _____ home at 8:00 in the morning.
　　　　　　　　6

Ken: What time (fly) _____ you _____?
　　　　　　　　　7　　　　　　　　8

Jim: At 9:30. I (have) _____ lunch with Carlos at 12:00 in San
　　　　　　　　　　9
Francisco.

Ken: Where (eat) _____ you _____?
　　　　　　　10　　　　　　　　　11

Jim: At the Blue Moon restaurant. Then I (go) _____ to the
　　　　　　　　　　　　　　　　　　　　　　12
office. I (work) _____ at the office until 5:00. Then I
　　　　　　　　　13
(meet) _____ Judy at 6:00.
　　　　　14

Ken: Where (go) _____ you _____?
               15   16

Jim: We (have) _____ dinner at the Prado restaurant. Dave
                  17

     (come) _____ , too.
                  18

Ken: That's a busy day. When (come) _____ you
                                   19

     _____ back?
               20

Jim: I (catch) _____ a flight at 9:30.
                  21

12 Your Turn

Work with a partner. Ask and answer questions about today and tomorrow.

Example:
You: Where are you going after class?
Your partner: I'm going to the library.

1. Where are you going after class?
2. How are you getting there?
3. What time are you leaving home tomorrow?
4. Are you meeting anyone today or tomorrow?
5. What are you doing this evening?

3e   The Simple Present Tense to Express Future Time

Function

School **starts** on January 8th.
The semester **ends** on June 5th.

We use the simple present for the future when it is part of a timetable or planned on a calendar.

The flight **arrives** at 10:30 tomorrow.
The train from the airport **leaves** at 11:00.

13 Practice

Look at today's program for a school group's trip to Disney World. Use the verbs from the list to write about their day. Use the verb *have* two times. Use the simple present tense.

arrive   depart   have   leave   return   take

Dear Parents:
      Here is the schedule for your child's trip to Disney World on Saturday, May 1.

8:00	Take the bus to Disney World
11:30	Arrive at Disney World
12:00	Lunch
1:00	Tour of Disney World
5:30	Depart for home
6:00	Sandwiches and drinks on the bus
9:00	Arrive at school

_____   _____
Date   Signature

1. _The children leave for Disney World_ _____ at 8:00.
2. _They_ _____ at 11:30.
3. _____ at 12:00.
4. _____ from 1:00 to 5:00.
5. _____ at 5:30.
6. _____ at 6:00.
7. _____ at 9:00.

14 Practice

Complete the sentences with the simple present or the present progressive of the verbs in parentheses.

1. This afternoon, I (watch) _____am watching_____ television. The big game
                                                              1
   (start) _____ at noon. Then my favorite quiz show
                         2
   (begin) _____ at 4:00.
                      3
2. The final exam (start) _____ at 10:00 tomorrow and
                                              4
   (end) _____ at 12:00.
                   5
3. My flight (arrive) _____ at 3:30 tomorrow, and then I
                                      6
   (take) _____ a taxi to the hotel.
                   7

4. The bank (open) _____ at 9:00 in the morning and

$\quad$ $\underset{8}{}$

$\quad$ (close) _____ at 5:00 in the afternoon.

$\quad$ $\underset{9}{}$

5. I (have) _____ dinner with Ben tonight. We

$\quad$ $\underset{10}{}$

$\quad$ (meet) _____ after work.

$\quad$ $\underset{11}{}$

6. Jenny (leave) _____ her job at the end of the week. She

$\quad$ $\underset{12}{}$

$\quad$ (take) _____ a vacation before she looks for another one.

$\quad$ $\underset{13}{}$

7. I (buy) _____ a new car this week. Then I

$\quad$ $\underset{14}{}$

$\quad$ (drive) _____ to Canada for my vacation.

$\quad$ $\underset{15}{}$

8. Do you remember that I (give) _____ a birthday party for

$\quad$ $\underset{16}{}$

$\quad$ Sandy? (come) _____ you _____?

$\quad$ $\underset{17}{}$ $\qquad$ $\underset{18}{}$

3f The Future Conditional

If I **go** to the library, I**'ll study.**
If I **study** hard, I**'ll pass** the test.

1. A conditional sentence has a main clause and a dependent clause that starts with *if*. The *if* clause expresses a condition. The main clause gives the result. Conditional sentences about future events or situations use the simple present tense in the *if* clause and the future tense in the main clause.

If Clause—Present Tense	Main Clause—Future Tense
If I **study** hard,	I **will pass** the test.
If you **don't study,**	you **will fail.**
If he **fails,**	his parents **won't give** him any money.
If we **don't go** out,	we**'ll have** more time to study.
If they **don't pass,**	they**'ll repeat** the class.

69

2. An *if* clause can come before or after the main clause. The meaning is the same. When the *if* clause comes first, we put a comma (,) after it.

> **If you don't study,** you will fail.
> You will fail **if you don't study.**

3. We use future conditional sentences to talk about events or situations that can possibly happen in the future.

> If I see Yuko tomorrow, I'll borrow her notes.
> If she gets an A, she'll be very happy.

---

15 Practice

Write sentences about what Katerina and Paolo hope will happen in the future. Use the result of one sentence as the condition of the next. Use results from the lists that make sense.

Katerina

become a dentist	pass her high school exams
earn a lot of money	study dentistry
go to the university	study more

Condition	**Result**
1. If she doesn't go out before the test,	she'll study more.
2. *If she studies more,*	she'll _____
3. _____	_____
4. _____	_____
5. _____	_____
6. _____	_____

Paolo

buy other businesses	retire when he's thirty-five
get a job	save money
make a lot of money	start his own business

Condition	**Result**
1. If he graduates this year,	he'll get a job.
2. _____	_____
3. _____	_____
4. _____	_____
5. _____	_____
6. _____	_____

Practice

Work with a partner. Ask and answer questions about Katerina and Paolo.

Example:
You: What will Katerina do if she goes to the university?
Your partner: She'll study dentistry.

3g   Future Time Clauses

We'll walk on Tower Bridge
before we go to Big Ben.

After we walk on Tower Bridge,
we'll go to Big Ben.

1. A future time clause can begin with conjunctions such as *before, after, as soon as,* or *when.* We usually use the simple present, not *will* or *going to,* in the time clause.

FUTURE TIME CLAUSE			MAIN CLAUSE	
Conjunction	Subject	Simple Present Tense Verb	Subject	Future Tense Verb
Before	I	**go** to London,	I	**will get** some British money.
When	she	**goes** to London,	she	**will spend** a lot.
After	they	**visit** the sights,	they	**will go** shopping.
As soon as	we	**arrive,**	we	**will call** you.

2. A future time clause is a dependent clause. It must be used with a main clause.

   CORRECT: When I get there, I will call you.
   INCORRECT: ~~When I get there.~~

3. We can put the time clause before or after the main clause. They both have the same meaning. When the time clause comes first, we put a comma after it.

As soon as we arrive, we'll call you.
We'll call you **as soon as we arrive.**

17 Practice

Anne and Paul are planning a trip to London. Complete the sentences with the correct form of the verbs in parentheses.

1. They (get) _____ *will get* _____ some traveler's checks before they
   (leave) _____ *leave* _____.

2. Anne (make) _____ a list of all the interesting places to
   visit before they (go) _____.

3. When they (get) _____ to London, they
   (stay) _____ at the Clifton Hotel. It's a small hotel in
   the center of London.

4. As soon as they (arrive) _____ at the hotel, they
   (call) _____ us.

5. When they (be) _____ in London, they
   (not, go) _____ to other towns.

6. They (not, have) _____ time to see everything before
   they (leave) _____.

7. After they (visit) _____ the sites, they
   (go) _____ shopping.

8. When they (walk) _____ around London, they
   (take) _____ photos.

9. They (take) _____ the subway or the bus when they
   (visit) _____ places.

10. When they (get) _____ tired, they
    (take) _____ a taxi.

11. After they (walk) _____ on Tower Bridge, they
    (go) _____ to see Big Ben, the clock.

12. When they (be) _____ hungry, they
    (eat) _____ some fish and chips.

13. If it (rain) _____ hard, they

(visit) _____ the British Museum.

14. When they (leave) _____ the hotel in the morning,

they (take) _____ their umbrellas with them.

15. After they (see) _____ Big Ben, they

(buy) _____ tickets to see a play.

16. If they (not, get) _____ tickets to the theater, they

(go) _____ to the ballet.

17. If they (have) _____ any time left, they

(take) _____ a ride on a boat on the river.

18. When Anne (go) _____ shopping, she

(spend) _____ a lot of money.

19. She (buy) _____ an English teapot when she

(see) _____ one.

20. They (get) _____ lots of souvenirs before they

(leave) _____.

18 Practice

Find the errors in the sentences and rewrite them correctly. If a sentences has no errors, write *No change*.

1. If I get some time off this winter, I go to Arizona for a vacation.

If I get some time off this winter, I will go to Arizona

for a vacation.

2. It will be warm, when I get to Phoenix.

_____

3. As soon as I will arrive, I will put on light clothes and walk in the sun.

_____

4. After I visit the sights in Phoenix I will rent a car and drive to the Grand Canyon.

_____

5. I take a lot of pictures as soon as I will get there.

_____

6. I will hike to the bottom of the canyon if I have time.

_____

7. When I get back to Phoenix I will play golf for a day or two.

_____

8. Before I will leave, I visit the Heard Museum.

_____

9. When I get on the airplane to go home, I will think, "It's going to be cold in Chicago!"

_____

19 Your Turn

Make predictions for the next five years about a famous person or yourself.

Example:
Madonna will have another baby.

20 Your Turn

Tell your partner three things that you think will happen in your future.
Use sentences with future time clauses.

Example:
After I finish this course, I'll look for a good job.

21 Your Turn

Work with a partner. Think of three superstitions. Tell them to the class using _if_ and the future tense.

Example:
In my country, if you see a black cat, you will have bad luck.

Write a paragraph about the city of the future.

Step 1. Work with a partner. Ask and answer questions about the city of the future. Write the answers. These prompts may help you.

  1. What kind of buildings will it have?
  2. What kind of transportation will people use?
  3. What kind of weather will it have?
  4. What kind of places for sports will it have?
  5. How will they control crime?
  6. Will there be animals?
  7. Will people live and work in the same city?
  8. Will there be stores?
  9. Will people go to restaurants?
 10. Will people go to movies?
 11. How clean will the city be?
 12. What kind of people will live in this city?

Step 2. Rewrite your answers in paragraph form. Write a title in a few words (The City of the Future). For more writing guidelines, see pages 199–203.

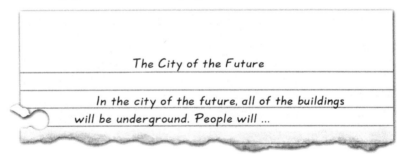

The City of the Future

In the city of the future, all of the buildings will be underground. People will ...

Step 3. Evaluate your paragraph.

Checklist

_____ Did you indent the first line?

_____ Did you give your paragraph a title?

_____ Did you put the title in the middle of the page?

_____ Did you capitalize the title correctly?

Step 4. Edit your work. Work with a partner or your teacher to edit your sentences. Correct spelling, punctuation, vocabulary, and grammar.

Step 5. Write your final copy.

SELF-TEST

A **Choose the best answer, A, B, C, or D, to complete the sentence. Mark your answer by darkening the oval with the same letter.**

1. I _____ with the administrator at 3:00 this afternoon.

   A. will going to meet   Ⓐ Ⓑ Ⓒ Ⓓ
   B. going meet
   C. am going to meet
   D. will to meet

2. They _____ to finish the construction next year.

   A. intend   Ⓐ Ⓑ Ⓒ Ⓓ
   B. are going to intend
   C. will intend
   D. intending

3. She'll call me when she _____ at the airport.

   A. will arrive   Ⓐ Ⓑ Ⓒ Ⓓ
   B. is arriving
   C. is going to arrive
   D. arrives

4. People _____ gasoline cars in the future.

   A. won't drive probably   Ⓐ Ⓑ Ⓒ Ⓓ
   B. are going to probably not drive
   C. probably won't drive
   D. are not driving probably

5. The bank _____ at ten o'clock.

   A. will to open   Ⓐ Ⓑ Ⓒ Ⓓ
   B. open
   C. going to open
   D. opens

6. Before I take the test tomorrow, I _____ my notes.

   A. review   Ⓐ Ⓑ Ⓒ Ⓓ
   B. do reviewing
   C. will review
   D. will to review

7. If it snows tomorrow, we _____ problems.

   A. are having   Ⓐ Ⓑ Ⓒ Ⓓ
   B. had
   C. have
   D. will have

8. I leave for Bangkok tomorrow. The conference _____ on Monday.

   A. starts   Ⓐ Ⓑ Ⓒ Ⓓ
   B. going to start
   C. will start
   D. starting

9. In the future, people _____ in underground cities.

   A. will live   Ⓐ Ⓑ Ⓒ Ⓓ
   B. live
   C. are living
   D. going to live

10. Architects _____ the plan will not have any problems.

   A. will hope   Ⓐ Ⓑ Ⓒ Ⓓ
   B. hoping
   C. are hope
   D. hope

B Find the underlined word or phrase, A, B, C, or D, that is incorrect. Mark your answer by darkening the oval with the same letter.

1. NASA <u>be</u> <u>planning</u> <u>to send</u> astronauts
         A   B   C

    <u>to</u> Mars in this century.
    D

    Ⓐ Ⓑ Ⓒ Ⓓ

2. <u>The scientists</u> <u>will</u> <u>hope</u> <u>to build</u> a space
        A   B   C   D

    station to orbit the earth in the future.

    Ⓐ Ⓑ Ⓒ Ⓓ

3. If <u>the United States</u> <u>will build</u> the space
          A   B

    station, <u>it</u> <u>will be</u> called *The Eagle*.
          C   D

    Ⓐ Ⓑ Ⓒ Ⓓ

4. You <u>won't</u> <u>be able</u> to vote <u>if</u> you <u>will</u> not
         A   B   C   D

    register by tomorrow.

    Ⓐ Ⓑ Ⓒ Ⓓ

5. <u>Scientists</u> <u>are</u> <u>probably</u> be able to predict
       A   B   C

    <u>earthquakes</u> in the future.
        D

    Ⓐ Ⓑ Ⓒ Ⓓ

6. <u>In the future</u>, people <u>are going</u> to the
         A   B

    moon <u>for</u> <u>their</u> vacations.
       C   D

    Ⓐ Ⓑ Ⓒ Ⓓ

7. He <u>is going to</u> celebrate <u>after</u> he <u>will get</u>
        A   B   C

    a good score <u>on</u> the test.
              D

    Ⓐ Ⓑ Ⓒ Ⓓ

8. Scientists <u>think</u> <u>transportation</u> <u>is</u> much
            A   B   C

    faster <u>in the future</u>.
         D

    Ⓐ Ⓑ Ⓒ Ⓓ

9. In the future, <u>people</u> <u>are driving</u> <u>electric</u>
              A   B   C

    <u>cars</u>.
    D

    Ⓐ Ⓑ Ⓒ Ⓓ

10. The store <u>is opening</u> <u>at</u> 10:00 every
              A   B

    <u>morning</u> except <u>on</u> Sundays.
      C   D

    Ⓐ Ⓑ Ⓒ Ⓓ

UNIT 4

NOUNS, ARTICLES, AND QUANTITY

4a Singular and Plural Nouns

Ben works on **a farm.** He has **a dog** and **a horse.** He takes care of the **cows, chickens,** and **sheep.**

1. Nouns name people, places, and things.

2. Singular nouns refer to one thing. Plural nouns refer to two or more things. All nouns have a singular form. Many nouns also have plural forms, but some do not.

SINGULAR NOUNS

3. We often use the articles *a* or *an* in front of a singular noun. We use *a* with nouns that start with a consonant sound. Some consonant sounds are spelled with the letters *b, c, d, f, g, h, j, k, l, m, n, p, q, r, s, t, v, w, x, y,* and *z.*

   a hat   **a** dog   **a** farmer   **a** neighborhood

   a university (the *u* in university starts with a *y* sound)

   We use *an* when a word begins with a vowel sound. Some vowel sounds are spelled with the letters *a, e, i, o,* and *u.*

   an animal   **an** eye   **an** ice cream

   an uncle   **an** hour (the *h* in *hour* is silent)

4. *A* and *an* have the same meaning. They mean "one."

PLURAL NOUNS

5. Many nouns have plural forms. We do not use the articles *a* and *an* before plural nouns.

6. We form the plural of most nouns by adding –*s* to the singular form. Sometimes there are other spelling changes.

REGULAR PLURAL NOUNS		
Rule	Singular Noun	Plural Noun
Add –s to most nouns.	horse	horse**s**
Add –es to nouns ending in s, ss, sh, ch, and x.	bus	bus**es**
	glass	glass**es**
	dish	dish**es**
	watch	watch**es**
	box	box**es**
Nouns ending in a consonant + y: change y to i and add –es.	country	countr**ies**
	party	part**ies**
Nouns ending in a vowel + y: add –s.	boy	boy**s**
	key	key**s**
Nouns ending in f or fe: change f or fe to –ves.	life	li**ves**
	leaf	lea**ves**
Exceptions:	belief	belief**s**
	chief	chief**s**
	roof	roof**s**
Nouns ending in o: Some add –es.	echo	echo**es**
	hero	hero**es**
	potato	potato**es**
	tomato	tomato**es**
Some add –s.	piano	piano**s**
	photo	photo**s**
	radio	radio**s**
	zoo	zoo**s**
Some can add either –s or –es.	zero	zero**s**/zero**es**
	volcano	volcano**s**/volcano**es**
	tornado	tornado**s**/tornado**es**

7. Some nouns have irregular plural forms.

IRREGULAR PLURAL NOUNS	
Singular	Plural
man	**men**
woman	**women**
child	**children**
tooth	**teeth**
foot	**feet**
mouse	**mice**
goose	**geese**
fish	**fish**
sheep	**sheep**
deer	**deer**
species	**species**
ox	**oxen**

1 Practice

Complete the sentences with *a* or *an*.

1. I took my nephew to _____*a*_____ zoo last weekend.

2. We saw _____ elephant and her baby.

3. There were _____ zebra and _____ antelope.

4. We spent almost _____ hour watching the monkeys.

5. We saw _____ hippopotamus in _____ lake.

6. It was _____ huge animal!

7. There was _____ exhibit of snakes, and my nephew loved it.

8 We met _____ guide there. He learned about snakes at _____

   university in Florida.

9. My nephew wanted to hold _____ snake, and the guide said yes.

10. I let him do it. I'm _____ good uncle, aren't I?

11. We had _____ ice cream cone before we left.

2 Practice

Underline the nouns in the sentences. Write *S* if a noun is singular. Write *P* if it is plural.

1. There were a lot of <u>men</u>, <u>women</u>, and <u>children</u> in the <u>park</u>.
   P   P   P   S

2. It was beautiful. The leaves were changing color.

3. There were geese on the lake.

4. A man and a woman were in a boat on the lake.

5. They were paddling the boat with their feet.

6. I could see many fish in the lake.

7. Some kids were listening to their radio and dancing.

8. Others were riding their bicycles.

9. It was a beautiful day for a walk in the park.

3 Practice

Write the plurals of the following words under the correct headings.

baby	child	fox	lady	photo	sandwich	tomato
bird	city	half	leaf	piano	sheep	toy
bush	dress	hero	mouse	potato	table	wolf
category	fish	key	ox	radio	tax	zoo
cherry	foot	knife	peach	roof	thief	

-s	-es	-ies	-os	-oes	-ves	Irregular
birds	_bushes_	_babies_	_____	_____	_____	_____
_____	_____	_____	_____	_____	_____	_____
_____	_____	_____	_____	_____	_____	_____
_____	_____	_____	_____	_____	_____	_____
_____	_____	_____	_____	_____	_____	_____
	_____					_____

4 Practice

Complete the sentences with the plural form of the nouns in parentheses.

Don: Did you go shopping yesterday?

Carla: Yes, I did. I bought a lot of things because they were on sale.

Don: Oh, what did you buy?

Carla: I bought two (dress) __dresses__ , two (shirt) _____ ,
           1   2

three (scarf) _____ , and two (tie) _____ for you.
         3   4

Don: Did you buy anything for the house?

Carla: Yes, I bought two beautiful (dish) _____ , six (knife) _____ ,
              5   6

six (fork) _____ , and six (glass) _____ .
        7   8

Don: Wow! You sure bought a lot of things!

5 Your Turn

Look around the classroom. Write the plural names of things you see. Who found the most things?

chairs   _____   _____   _____

_____   _____   _____   _____

_____   _____   _____   _____

4b Nouns as Subjects, Objects, and Objects of Prepositions

Sheep eat **grass.**
Lambs are baby sheep.
The **lambs** are lying on the **grass.**

1. A noun can be the subject of a sentence. The subject names the thing or person that does the action in a sentence.

2. A noun can be the object of a verb. The object names the thing or person that receives the action of the verb.

3. A noun can be the object of a preposition. The object of a preposition is a noun or pronoun that follows a preposition. A preposition and the words following it are a prepositional phrase.

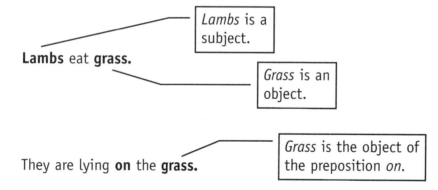

Lambs is a subject.

Lambs eat **grass.**

Grass is an object.

They are lying **on** the **grass.**

Grass is the object of the preposition *on*.

Some Prepositions

about	before	down	off	toward
above	behind	during	on	under
across	below	for	out	until
after	beside	from	over	up
against	besides	in	since	upon
among	between	into	through	with
around	beyond	near	throughout	within
at	by	of	to	without

Practice

Underline and label the subject (S), verb (V), and object (O) of each sentence.

      S   V O
1. The <u>farm</u> <u>has</u> <u>cows.</u>

2. The cows give milk.

3. The family drinks the milk.

4. The farm has chickens.

5. Don feeds the chickens.

6. The chickens lay eggs.

7. Don has a dog.

8. The dog follows Don.

9. His brother has a cat.

10. The cat hates the dog.

11. The cat chases the chickens.

Practice

Label the subject (S), verb (V), preposition (P), and the object of the preposition (OP).

     S   V P OP
1. <u>Ben</u> <u>lives</u> <u>on</u> a <u>farm.</u>

2. Ben wears a hat on the farm.

3. Ben works on the farm with his brother and father.

4. His mother cooks the food for the family.

5. His mother grows vegetables in a garden behind the farmhouse.

6. The family eats the vegetables from the garden.

7. The family drinks milk from the cows on the farm.

8. The family eats eggs from the chickens in the yard.

9. Ben drives his truck to the town on Saturdays.

10. Ben buys groceries from the store in town.

11. Ben takes his dog with him on the truck.

12. Ben and his dog come back to the farm for lunch.

13. His mother prepares lunch with fresh bread.

14. His mother makes the bread at home for the family.

4c Count Nouns and Noncount Nouns

Fresh **air** is good for your **health.**
Fresh **air** has a lot of **oxygen.**

1. Count nouns are nouns that we can count (one book, two books, three books, etc.). They can be singular or plural (a chair, two chairs).

2. We put *a* or *an* before singular nouns.

3. We cannot count noncount nouns. They have no plural.

4. We do not use the articles *a* or *an* with noncount nouns.

5. Some nouns that are usually noncount can also be count nouns, but the meaning is different.

NONCOUNT NOUN: She makes salad dressing with olive **oil.**
COUNT NOUN: She uses several **oils** in her cooking. (*Oils* = kinds of oil)

NONCOUNT NOUN: Brazil produces a lot of **coffee.**
COUNT NOUN: Can I buy you **a coffee?** (*A coffee* = a cup of coffee)

Here are some common noncount nouns in categories.

Categories	Examples of Noncount Nouns		
Solids	beef	glass	pasta
	bread	gold	plastic
	butter	ham	pork
	chalk	ice-cream	silk
	cheese	iron	soap
	chicken	margarine	steel
	coal	meat	wood
	cotton	nylon	wool
	fish	paper	yogurt
Liquids	beer	juice	soup
	blood	milk	tea
	coffee	oil	vinegar
	gasoline	shampoo	water
	honey	soda	wine
Powders and Grains	cereal	flour	salt
	corn	pepper	sand
	dust	rice	sugar
Gases	air	oxygen	smog
	fog	pollution	smoke
	hydrogen	smell	steam
Names of Categories	clothing	fruit	mail
	email	furniture	money
	food	jewelry	traffic
School Subjects and Languages	biology	Korean	music
	Chinese	literature	science
	history	math	Spanish
Weather	darkness	light	sunshine
	frost	rain	thunder
	hail	sleet	weather
	ice	snow	wind
Physical Forces	electricity	light	speed
	gravity	magnetism	weight

Categories	Examples of Noncount Nouns		
Abstract Nouns (things we cannot touch)	advice	health	love
	beauty	help	luck
	crime	homework	peace
	education	information	poverty
	fun	innocence	progress
	guilt	insurance	time
	happiness	kindness	wealth
	hate	knowledge	work

8 | Practice

Complete the paragraph with the singular or plural form of the nouns in parentheses. Use the singular form if the noun is a noncount noun. Use the plural form if the noun is a count noun.

When I go to the supermarket, I read all of the (label) _____*labels*_____. That
                                                              1
takes a lot of (time) _____. I don't eat frozen (food) _____.
                              2   3
I prefer fresh (fruit) _____ and (vegetable) _____.
                            4   5
I like (apple) _____, (banana) _____, and
                      6   7
(strawberry) _____. But the (vegetable) _____ are always
                    8   9
the same. There are always (potato) _____, (tomato) _____,
                                            10   11
and (carrot) _____. I also get (milk) _____,
                    12   13
(butter) _____, (cheese) _____, and
                14   15
(egg) _____. And (ice cream) _____, of course!
            16   17

9 | Your Turn

Agree or disagree with the statements below.

Examples:
Meat is good for you.
I agree. Meat is good for you.
I disagree. Meat is bad for you.

1. Meat is good for you.
2. Eggs are bad for you.
3. Sugar is good for you.

4. Coffee is bad for you.
5. Water is bad for you.

10 Your Turn

Write about what you eat.

Example:
For breakfast, I eat bread and jam. For lunch, I eat a sandwich and some fruit, and for dinner, I eat fish or chicken and some vegetables. I drink a lot of coffee and tea, but I never drink any soda.

11 Practice

Complete the sentences with the singular or plural of the nouns in parentheses.

A.

Today cars run on (gasoline) _____gasoline_____, but one day they will

1

run on (electricity) _____. Then there will be no more

2

(pollution) _____. The (air) _____ will be clean. There

3   4

won't be (smog) _____ or (smoke) _____ from

5   6

(car) _____ and other (traffic) _____.

7   8

B.

My new living room looks nice. There are no (rug) _____ on

1

the floor. The floor is made of (wood) _____. There is a lot of

2

(light) _____ in the room from the two big (window) _____.

3   4

I have two big (armchair) _____. They are covered in blue

5

(cotton) _____. The (furniture) _____ is all

6   7

new and modern. I have two small (table) _____ made of

8

(steel) _____ and (glass) _____, and there are two big

9   10

(lamp) _____.

11

C.

I need to get some (information) _____ about my
                                         1
(class) _____ next semester. I want to take (science) _____
                 2   3
subjects like (biology) _____ , (chemistry) _____ , and
                               4   5
(physics) _____ . Ben has a lot of (knowledge) _____ about
                   6   7
these things. He took these (course) _____ here last semester. He can give
                                              8
me (help) _____ and some good (advice) _____ , I'm sure.
                 9   10

12 Practice

Work with a partner. Write as many nouns as you can for the categories below. The
pair with the most correct is the winner.

1. Things you see on a farm

   __animals__   __fences__   _____   _____

2. Things you wear

   _____   _____   _____   _____

3. What things are made of

   _____   _____   _____   _____

4d A, An, and Some

There is **a** vase with **some** flowers
in it, **a** wallet, **some** keys on **a** key
chain, **a** pair of sunglasses, and
some mail.

1. We use *a* or *an* in front of singular count nouns.

   a book   **an** orange

2. We use *some* in front of noncount nouns. We don't use *a* or *an* in front of noncount nouns.

   CORRECT: I need **some** milk to make this cake.
   INCORRECT: I need ~~a milk~~* to make this cake.

3. We also use *some* with plural count nouns.

   a book   **some** books

   *It is possible to say "a milk," but the meaning is "a serving of milk."

13 Practice

What does Pete carry with him? Complete the sentences with *a, an,* or *some*.

I have _____*a*_____ wallet. In the wallet, there is _____ money, and there
  1   2
are _____ business cards. I also have _____ identification card,
        3   4
_____ check book, and _____ credit cards. In my pocket, I have
     5   6
_____ pen, _____ keys, _____ cell phone, and _____
     7   8   9   10
address book.

14 Practice

Nancy always carries a lot of things in her bag. Complete the sentence with *a, an,* or *some*.

She has _____*a*_____ hairbrush, _____ make-up bag, _____ coin
  1   2   3
purse, _____ wallet, _____ pack of tissues, _____ bottle of water,
           4   5   6
_____ pens, _____ apple, _____ umbrella, _____
     7   8   9   10
notepad, _____ paperclips, _____ calendar, _____ rubber bands,
              11   12   13
_____ jewelry, and _____ letters.
     14   15

Your Turn

Someone takes you to a restaurant. You can eat whatever you want. Don't think about diet or the price. Tell the class what you want to eat and drink.

Example:
I want a big steak with some French fries. I want some hot bread with some cheese. Then I'll have some ice cream with some strawberries and cream.

4e   *Some, Any, Much, Many, A Little, A Few,* and *A Lot Of*

Form / Function

A: Did you see **any** crocodiles at the zoo?
B: Yes, we saw **a few.**

	Affirmative	Negative
Count Nouns	There are **many** kangaroos.	There aren't **many** kangaroos.
	There are **a lot of** snakes.	There aren't **a lot of** snakes.
	There are **some** big towns.	There aren't **any** big towns.
	There are **a few** trees.	There aren't **many** trees.
Noncount Nouns	There is **a lot of** sunshine.	There isn't **much** sunshine.
	There is **some** rain.	There isn't **any** rain.
	There is **a little** snow.	There isn't **much** snow.

16 Practice

Ted and Julia went to Australia. Their friend is asking questions about their vacation. Circle the correct expression in parentheses.

Mary: Did you see a lot of wild animals? How about koala bears?

Ted: No, we didn't see ((any) / some) koala bears, but we saw (a little / a lot of)
                                    1   2
        kangaroos. They were everywhere in the countryside.

Mary: Did you stay in the cities or did you go to the countryside?

Ted: We didn't spend (a few / any) time in the city. We drove into a desert area called the
                        3
outback. You don't see (any / a few) people for hours, and of course there isn't
                                    4
(a few / any) traffic. There is (a lot of / any) sunshine, and there aren't
        5   6
(a few / any) trees. You see, there isn't (much / a few) water in this area. I'm
        7   8
glad we took (much / a lot of) water with us in bottles. There are (much / a few)
                9   10
farms. We met (any / a few) nice people, and someone took us to a river where there
                    11
are (a lot of / much) crocodiles. We saw (a few / any) crocodiles after ten minutes.
            12   13
I was really scared! Julia wanted to stay longer, but we didn't have (a lot of / a few)
                                                                                14
time and had to get back to the city and the airport. I have (any / a lot of) photos
                                                                        15
to show you.

17 Practice

Complete the sentences with *many, much, a few,* or *a little*. Some sentences have more than one correct answer.

I live in a small town in Australia. There aren't _____*many*_____ houses there.
                                                                1
There are _____ stores in the town, but they don't sell
                    2
_____ products. There aren't _____ things to see
            3   4
in the town, and there isn't _____ entertainment. There aren't
                                    5
_____ young people, and they go to the city on weekends to have
        6
_____ fun. The city is only _____ hours drive from the
        7   8
town, and there isn't _____ traffic on the way.
                                9

18 Your Turn

What do you do on Saturdays? Talk about your free time activities, the things you buy, etc. Make five sentences. Use *much, many, a lot of, a little,* and *a few*.

Example:
I have a lot of free time on Saturdays. I go out with a few friends. I do a little homework.

4f Few, A Few, Little, and A Little

He has **a few** cookies.

She has **few** cookies.

1. We use *few* and *a few* with plural count nouns (*books, tables*, etc.).

    A few means not many, but enough. It has a positive meaning.

    > I have **a few** apples. I can make an apple pie.

    Few means almost none. It has a negative meaning.

    > There are **few** apples. We must get some more.

2. We use *little* and *a little* with noncount nouns (*milk, time*, etc.).

    A little means not much, but enough.

    > I have **a little** time. I can finish this exercise.

    Little means almost none. It has a negative meaning.

    > I have **little** time. I must hurry.

---

19 Practice

Complete the sentences with *a few, few, a little*, or *little*.

1. Stella knew _____*little*_____ English before she took _____*a few*_____
    courses.

2. I like to listen to _____ music when I drive, especially
    _____ old Beatles songs.

3. There is _____ time before the train leaves, so we can buy

   _____ magazines and things from the store.

4. There's _____ food left in the refrigerator. I'll go to the supermarket

   and get _____ things.

5. A: Do you need _____ help?

   B: Yes, please. There are _____ questions I can't answer.

6. He's a strange man. I think he has _____ secrets.

   _____ people understand him.

7. I have _____ free time now. I'm very busy with my job, but there are

   _____ days when I don't have to work.

8. My mother sent me _____ money, so I am going to buy

   _____ things I need.

9. I bought _____ books. They were on sale. Everybody was buying them.

   There will be _____ books left now.

10. He knows _____ English, so he's going to take _____

    English classes.

11. Can you put _____ milk and _____ spoons of sugar

    on my cereal?

12. _____ students did not pass the test; they said they had

    _____ time.

13. I live _____ blocks from the train station, so there is

    _____ noise from the trains. Sometimes it wakes me up.

14. There are many pieces of furniture left on sale, but _____ are nice.

15. I have _____ problems. I need _____ advice.

16. I'd like _____ vegetables and _____ chicken, please.

17. We took _____ summer clothes with us, but we had

    _____ days of warm weather.

18. She's having a party and invited _____ friends over.

19. Are you hungry? There's _____ milk and _____ cookies.

20. She lost _____ points on the test because she was

    _____ minutes late.

4g   Units of Measure with Nouns

A: What's in the grocery bags?
B: There's **a bag of** potato chips, **a loaf of** bread, **a bunch of** celery, and many other things.

1. We use units of measure such as *a cup of coffee* or *a glass of water* to express quantities of noncount nouns and count nouns.

2. Count nouns following the units of measure are plural.

3. Here are some units of measure.

a bag of chips	a head of lettuce	a sheet of paper
a bar of soap	a jar of jam	a slice of cake
a bottle of water	a loaf of bread	a tube of toothpaste
a box of chocolates	a package of spaghetti	two pounds of apples/cheese
a bunch of bananas	a piece of fruit	ten gallons of gasoline
a can of tomatoes/soup	a piece of information	two cartons of milk
a carton of milk/juice	a roll of toilet paper	two cups of tea

20 Practice

Pam wrote a note for Pete. Complete the note with the following quantity words.

a bag of   a tube of
a bar of   bottles of
a bunch of   cartons of
a can of   pounds of
a loaf of   sheets of
a pound of

Shopping List

Pete,

I'll be home late. Can you go to the store for me? Here's a list.

2 _cartons of_ milk
a loaf of bread
_____ cheese
3 _____ water
_____ toothpaste
2 _____ red apples
_____ bananas
_____ vegetable soup
_____ potato chips
_____ soap
100 _____ paper for my computer

---

21 Your Turn

Work with a partner. Look at the following shopping list. Ask questions with *how much* or *how many* for each item. Answer with quantity expressions such as numbers, *some, a lot of, a few,* and *a little.*

Example:
soap
A: How much soap do you need?
B: Not much. two bars.

Shopping List

apples	margarine
bread	oranges
chips	potatoes
honey	rice
juice	soap
lettuce	vitamin C
light bulbs	yogurt

4h Possessive Nouns

My uncle**'s** name is Jim.
He's in the photo, and
that's Jim**'s** son, Tommy.

1. We use *'s* (apostrophe + *s*) or *'* (apostrophe) to talk about things that belong to people.

Singular Possessive Noun	Plural Possessive Noun
My uncle**'s** name is Jim. (one uncle)	My uncles**'** names are Jim and Ken. (more than one uncle)
It's the boy**'s** bag. (one boy)	They are the boys**'** bags. (more than one boy)
This is the girl**'s** room. (one girl)	This is the girls**'** room. (more than one girl)

2. We add *'s* or just *'* for names and nouns that end in *–s*.

   This is James**'s** friend. OR This is James**'** friend.
   That is the boss**'s** car. OR That is the boss**'** car.

3. We use *'s* with irregular plurals.

   These are the children**'s** books.
   They sell women**'s** clothes.
   That's a men**'s** store.

22 Practice

Add *'s* or *'* to the underlined nouns to show possession.

Rita: Where did you take this photo?

Laura: At my ___friend's___ house. My ___friend___ name is Carla. That day was the
             1   2

   ___twins___ birthday party. This is Cindy, my ___brother___ wife. And that is
        3   4

   ___Cindy___ sister.
         5

Rita: Who are the two boys?

Laura: The ___boys___ names are Ken and Dave. They are ___Cindy___ sons. And that's the
              6   7
        ___boys___ teacher, Mrs. Parkinson.
              8

23 Practice

Rewrite these questions using possessive nouns.

1. What's the first name of your father?

   What's your father's first name? _____

2. What are the names of your friends?

   _____

3. What's the name of your mother?

   _____

4. What are the colors of the shirts of the women in your class?

   _____

5. What are some of the favorite movies of your classmates?

   _____

6. What's the telephone number of your doctor?

   _____

7. What are the colors of the shoes of the men in your class?

   _____

24 Your Turn

Write answers to the questions in Practice 23.

1. My *father's first name is Frank.* _____

2. My _____

3. My _____

4. In class, the _____

5. My _____

6. My _____

7. In class, the _____

4i   *A, An,* or *The*

There is **a** woman outside. She is sitting on **a** truck. **The** truck is big and old. **The** woman is young.

1. We use *a* or *an* when we talk about a person or a thing (singular count noun) for the first time. We use *the* when we talk about it for the second time.

    There is **a** woman outside. **The** woman is sitting on **a** truck.

2. We use *a* or *an* when we talk about a general, not a specific, person or thing.

    I spent **a** year in Mexico City.

3. We use *the* when the person we are speaking to knows which person or thing we are talking about.

    Ted: Where's Bill?
    Annie: He's in **the** house.
    (Both Ted and Annie know which house they are talking about.)

4. We use *the* with count nouns (singular and plural) and noncount nouns.

    She has a truck. **The** truck is old. (singular count noun)
    I ate two cookies. **The** cookies were delicious. (plural count noun)
    We had some coffee. **The** coffee was good. (noncount noun)

25 Practice

Complete the sentences with *a, an,* or *the.*

A.

Kelly had ___a___ pain in her back, so she went to _____ doctor that her friend
          1   2

recommended. _____ doctor gave her _____ tablet to take every day. After _____ few
               3   4   5

days, _____ pain went away.
     6

B.

I gave Lucy _____ gift for her ninth birthday. It was _____ box of paints. Now she
           1   2

spends _____ hour or more every day painting. She wants to be _____ artist one day.
       3   4

Yesterday, she painted _____ picture of _____ woman. _____ painting is very good. She
                  5   6   7

is going to give it to _____ friend.
          8

C.

I live in _____ apartment in Boston. It is _____ old apartment building in _____
       1   2   3

center of _____ city. There is _____ elevator and _____ doorman at _____ entrance of
      4   5   6   7

the building. I have _____ view from my kitchen window. _____ apartment is nice, but
            8   9

it is hot in _____ summer.
     10

D.

Yesterday was _____ very bad day. I had a lot of work at _____ office. On the way
          1   2

back, I missed my train and took _____ taxi. When I arrived home, there was _____
                       3   4

message from _____ friend on my answering machine. She told me to meet her at _____
        5   6

restaurant at seven. She gave me _____ name of the restaurant and its address. I went
                      7

to _____ restaurant, but she wasn't there. I waited for _____ hour and came back home.
   8   9

I was hungry, tired, and in _____ bad mood.
                    10

4j Generalizations

Giraffes live in Africa.
Giraffes are tall.
Giraffes have long necks.
Giraffes eat leaves.

1. We do not use *the* when we talk about something in general.

   Giraffes are tall.
   Diamonds are expensive.
   I love **fish.**

2. We use *the* when we talk about specific things.

   The giraffes that we saw at the zoo were beautiful.
   The diamond in your ring is beautiful.
   The fish that you made last night was delicious.

26 Practice

Complete the sentences with *the* or *X* (no article).

1. Drinkable __*X*__ water is more expensive than __*X*__ salt in some parts of the
   world.

2. _____ water that we drink in this city is not good. Many people buy _____ water in
   bottles.

3. She loves _____ coffee. She drank all _____ coffee in the pot.

4. Which is more important for you, _____ love or _____ money?

5. I love _____ photographs, and I really like _____ photographs you took of Rome.

6. You know, _____ cars can't run without _____ gas.

7. Although _____ formal education is important, _____ education you get at home is just as important.

8. I think that _____ money is important. Where is _____ money I gave you yesterday?

9. Did you know that _____ oranges have Vitamin C? _____ oranges we had this morning were very sweet.

10. Do you know that _____ glass is made from _____ sand?

11. They say that _____ time is _____ money. I will never forget _____ time I spent in Singapore with you.

12. We studied _____ French at school, but _____ French we studied was not very natural.

13. I think that _____ watches are not so expensive today. Most watches today work on _____ batteries.

14. In this city, _____ museums are closed on Mondays, but _____ Museum of Science is open this Monday for a special exhibit.

15. I learned that _____ land animals don't live in Antarctica. Only _____ seals and _____ penguins can live there.

16. It's true that _____ life is very difficult without _____ electricity.

17. It's a fact that _____ doctors make more money than _____ teachers.

18. I like working with _____ people, and _____ people in this department are wonderful.

19. We all have _____ problems. Helen told me about _____ problems she has at work.

20. Don is a vegetarian. He doesn't eat _____ meat, but he eats _____ eggs and _____ cheese.

27 Practice

Complete the sentences with *the, a, an,* or *X* (no article).

John gave Linda __X__ flowers for her birthday. It was _____ hot day, and _____
         1   2   3

flowers looked terrible by the time he gave them to her. He also bought _____ chocolates
                                                                     4

for her. He put _____ chocolates in _____ car, and when she opened _____ box, they
               5   6   7

were warm and soft. Then he took her to _____ movie. _____ movie was a horror film.
                                          8   9

John forgot Linda didn't like _____ horror movies. _____ movie was frightening. At the
                              10   11

end of _____ movie, John heard _____ scream. He thought it was _____ woman in
         12   13   14

_____ movie, but it was Linda.
 15

28 Your Turn

Say five things you like and five things you don't like. Use the ideas from the list or your own.

Example:
I like cats, but I don't like their hair.

soccer   classical music   modern art
chocolates   horror movies   rock music

WRITING: Write a Friendly Letter

Complete a letter to a friend about a vacation.

Step 1. Work with a partner. Think of a famous vacation place. It may be anywhere in the world. Ask and answer questions about this place. Write your answers. Answer the questions using *some, any, a lot of, much, many, a,* and *the.*

Ask questions like these:
What kinds of things did you see?
What photos did you take?
What kinds of things did you eat?
What gifts or souvenirs did you buy?

Step 2. Rewrite your answers as a paragraph to complete a letter like this one. For more writing guidelines, see pages 199–203.

August 18, 20XX

Dear Hamid,
    You were right. Alex and I had a fantastic time at the pyramids in Egypt. Everyone should go there at least once.

    When we were there, we saw _____
_____
_____
_____
_____

    Thanks again for your advice. I'm telling all of my friends that they must visit the Egyptian pyramids. It was the best vacation I've ever had.

    Your friend,
    Julio

Step 3. Evaluate your paragraph.

Checklist

_____ Did you indent the first line?

_____ Did you describe your experiences on your vacation?

_____ Did you use articles and quantifying words like *many, much, some, any, a, an,* and *the?*

Step 4. Edit your work. Work with a partner to edit your sentences. Correct spelling, punctuation, vocabulary, and grammar.

Step 5. Write your final copy.

SELF-TEST

A   Choose the best answer, A, B, C, or D, to complete the sentence. Mark your answer by darkening the oval with the same letter.

1. There is _____ at this time.

    A. many traffic   Ⓐ Ⓑ Ⓒ Ⓓ
    B. a lot of traffic
    C. lot of traffic
    D. traffics

2. Did you see _____ kangaroos in Australia?

    A. much   Ⓐ Ⓑ Ⓒ Ⓓ
    B. a
    C. a little
    D. any

3. We need _____ from the supermarket.

    A. a loaf of bread   Ⓐ Ⓑ Ⓒ Ⓓ
    B. a piece of bread
    C. a bread
    D. a packet of bread

4. There are _____ tourists in small towns.

    A. few   Ⓐ Ⓑ Ⓒ Ⓓ
    B. any
    C. little
    D. much

5. The price of a _____ of lettuce is going up again.

    A. piece   Ⓐ Ⓑ Ⓒ Ⓓ
    B. bar
    C. bunch
    D. head

6. It's bedtime. Can you turn off _____?

    A. a light   Ⓐ Ⓑ Ⓒ Ⓓ
    B. the light
    C. light
    D. lights

7. I have _____ on me.

    A. a money   Ⓐ Ⓑ Ⓒ Ⓓ
    B. few money
    C. a little money
    D. a few money

8. These are _____ toys.

    A. the children's   Ⓐ Ⓑ Ⓒ Ⓓ
    B. the children
    C. the childrens'
    D. the childrens

9. In this town, there is _____.

    A. an university   Ⓐ Ⓑ Ⓒ Ⓓ
    B. a university
    C. the university
    D. university

10. In _____, the police don't carry guns.

    A. some country   Ⓐ Ⓑ Ⓒ Ⓓ
    B. some countries
    C. some country's
    D. some countries'

B   Find the underlined word or phrase, A, B, C, or D, that is incorrect. Mark your answer by darkening the oval with the same letter.

1. Everyday <u>life</u> is <u>difficult</u> without <u>an</u>
        A   B   C
<u>electricity</u>.
    D

Ⓐ Ⓑ Ⓒ Ⓓ

2. There <u>are</u> <u>a lot of</u> <u>sheeps</u> <u>in</u> New Zealand.
         A   B   C   D

Ⓐ Ⓑ Ⓒ Ⓓ

3. Could <u>you</u> please <u>give</u> me <u>some</u> <u>advices</u>?
            A   B   C   D

Ⓐ Ⓑ Ⓒ Ⓓ

4. He needs <u>any</u> <u>help</u> <u>with</u> <u>his</u> <u>homework</u>.
               A   B   C   D

Ⓐ Ⓑ Ⓒ Ⓓ

5. <u>The grass</u> looks <u>green</u> today because
        A   B
<u>we got</u> <u>any</u> rain this week.
    C   D

Ⓐ Ⓑ Ⓒ Ⓓ

6. <u>A pollution</u> is <u>a</u> problem in many large
        A   B
<u>cities</u> <u>in the United States</u>.
    C   D

Ⓐ Ⓑ Ⓒ Ⓓ

7. <u>Some</u> people <u>say</u> that <u>the money</u> cannot
        A   B   C
buy <u>happiness</u>.
        D

Ⓐ Ⓑ Ⓒ Ⓓ

8. California has <u>a good weather</u>, but
                     A
<u>there are</u> <u>a lot of</u> <u>earthquakes</u>.
    B   C   D

Ⓐ Ⓑ Ⓒ Ⓓ

9. <u>Vegetarians</u> don't eat <u>meats</u>, and some
        A   B
don't eat <u>eggs</u> or <u>cheese</u>.
              C   D

Ⓐ Ⓑ Ⓒ Ⓓ

10. Could I have <u>some</u> <u>informations</u> about
                    A   B
<u>the courses</u> <u>for next semester</u>?
    C   D

Ⓐ Ⓑ Ⓒ Ⓓ

Nouns, Articles, and Quantity

UNIT 5

PRONOUNS

5a   Subject and Object Pronouns

At the moment, **he** doesn't like **her**, and **she** doesn't like **him. They** are angry.

1. Many sentences in English have a subject, a verb, and an object. The subject and the object can be nouns.

Subject (Noun)	Verb	Object (Noun)
Mike	plays	**football** very well.
Helena and Joe	love	**their children.**

2. We can replace nouns with pronouns.

Subject (Pronoun)	Verb	Object (Pronoun)
He	plays	**it** very well.
They	love	**them.**

3. Pronouns used as subjects are sometimes different from pronouns used as objects.

Subject Pronouns	Object Pronouns
I	me
you	you
he	him
she	her
it	it
we	us
they	them

4. A pronoun can refer to a noun or to a noun phrase (a noun + a group of words related to the noun).

Subject (Noun)	Verb	Object (Noun Phrase)	Subject (Pronoun)	Verb	Object (Pronoun)	
Lisa	drives	**an old black car.**	**She**	bought	**it**	last year.

5. We use object pronouns after prepositions.

Subject	Verb	Prepositional Phrase (Noun Phrase Object)	Subject (Pronoun)	Verb	Prepositional Phrase (Pronoun Object)
We	listened	to **the math teacher.**	**We**	listened	**to him.**

6. Remember to use the correct pronoun forms.

CORRECT: My friends and I went to the mall.
INCORRECT: My friends and ~~me~~ went to the mall.

CORRECT: Sam saw my friends and me at the mall.
INCORRECT: Sam saw my friends and ~~I~~ at the mall.

CORRECT: I went to the mall with you and him.
INCORRECT: I went to the mall with you and ~~he.~~

---

1   Practice

Complete the sentences with a subject or an object pronoun.

1. Eddy likes football, but I don't like _____*it*_____.

2. As for me, _____ like tennis, but Eddy doesn't like _____.

3. Eddy's favorite movie star is Arnold Schwarzenegger, but I don't like _____ very much.

4. He also likes Britney Spears, but I don't like _____.

5. My favorite movie stars are Jodie Foster and Mel Gibson, but Eddy doesn't like _____.

6. My friends and _____ are going shopping, but Eddy doesn't want to come with _____.

7. Eddy likes _____, but I don't like him.

8. Why do I talk about _____ so much?

2 Practice

Complete the sentences with subject and object pronouns.

A.

I am a student at a university. I am studying computer science. _____*It*_____ is a

good subject. My friend, Tom, is taking the same courses with _____.

_____ do our homework together in the library. I like the library. _____ is

a quiet place. Tom and _____ have our final examinations next week. I want to

pass _____. Then my parents will buy a motorcycle for _____.

B.

I work for Mr. Kim on Saturdays. I help _____ in his store and he pays

_____ money. I am saving _____ to buy my mother a necklace.

_____ is going to be very happy. _____ is going to be a surprise

for _____.

C.

My mother can't find her glasses. _____ is looking for _____ all over

the house. She says she put _____ on the table in the kitchen, and now

_____ are not there. She says she can't drive without _____. My father

has to drive _____ to work tomorrow.

D.

Mike: Is Maria coming to the party?

Ken: I invited _____, but I don't know if _____ will come. Her

parents are visiting, and she may take _____ somewhere.

Mike: What about Bill? Did you invite _____ when you saw him yesterday?

Ken: Yes, he is coming with Janet. _____ will both come.

Mike: Oh no! Not Janet! I really don't want to see _____.

Your Turn

Talk or write about two gifts you gave or received recently.

Example:
My father gave me a computer for my birthday last year. I love it.

5b   Possessive Adjectives and Possessive Pronouns

Form / Function

A: Is this **your** key?
B: No, it isn't **mine.**

Possessive Adjectives	Possessive Pronouns
my	mine
your	yours
his	his
her	hers
its	its*
our	ours
their	theirs

*We rarely need to use the possessive pronoun *its*.

1. We put a possessive adjective before a noun. We use a possessive pronoun alone. There is no noun after it.

   This is **my** key. It's **mine.**
   That is **their** car. It's **theirs.**
   Their car is blue. **Mine** is red.

2. We use possessive adjectives and possessive pronouns to show that something belongs to somebody.

> Excuse me, is this **your** pen? OR Excuse me, is this pen **yours?**

3. Be careful when using *its/it's* and *their/they're*. They are pronounced the same but their meanings are different.

Word	Meaning	Example
its	Possessive form of *it*.	It's a great car, but I don't like **its** color.
it's	Contraction of *it is*.	Where's the car? **It's** in the garage.
their	Possessive adjective of *they*.	**Their** car has a flat tire.
they're	Contraction of *they are*.	**They're** getting it fixed now.
there	Shows location	The car is in the garage. It's safe **there.**
	Shows existence	**There** is a problem with my car.

4 Practice

Underline the correct word.

A.

Paolo: Is this (<u>your</u>/yours) wallet?
           1

Lillian: No, it's not (mine/my). I thought it was (your/yours).
               2   **3**

Paolo: No, I have (my/mine) in my pocket. Maybe (its/it's) Ingrid's.
              4   **5**

Lillian: If it is (her/hers), she will be very worried. She went to the airport with
             6

     (her/hers) husband. He came to pick (her/she) up in (his/him) car. They
      7   **8**   **9**

     went to meet (her/hers) parents. (They're/Their) coming from Canada to stay
                 10   **11**

     with (them/they) for the holidays.
         12

B.

     (Our/Ours) television is not working. (Our/Ours) neighbors have an extra
      1   **2**

television, and (they're/there) going to give (it/its) to (us/we). We have to fix
              3   **4**   **5**

(our/ours) or get a new one. (They're/Their) expensive, you know. Our neighbors don't
  6   **7**

mind, so we may watch (theirs/their) for a long time.
                  8

C.

The Parkers are (our/ours) neighbors. (They're/Their) very rich. They have two cars in
    ₁   ₂

(theirs/their) garage, and the Porsche parked in front of (our/ours) house is (their/theirs),
    ₃   ₄   ₅

too. Everybody thinks (its/it's) (our/ours), but (our/ours) is an old Honda. We park it in
                        ₆   ₇   ₈

front of (our/ours) other neighbor's house. We like to leave it (their/there).
        ₉   ₁₀

---

5 | **Your Turn**

Discuss three things about your neighbor's house, apartment, or car, and your house, apartment, or car.

Example:
Our neighbor's apartment is dark. Ours is sunny.

5c   Reflexive Pronouns

Form

She's looking at **herself** in the mirror.

Subject Pronouns	Reflexive Pronouns
I	myself
you (singular)	yourself
he	himself
she	herself
it	itself
we	ourselves
you (plural)	yourselves
they	themselves

1. We use reflexive pronouns as objects when the subject and the object of the verb or preposition refer to the same person or thing.

Subject	Verb	Object
She	hurt	**herself.**
The machine	can't work	by **itself.**

2. Reflexive pronouns often come after these verbs and phrases.

be proud of	enjoy	take care of
behave	help*	talk to
burn	hurt	teach
cut	introduce	work for

*If you *help yourself to something*, it means "serve yourself something."
For example, "Help yourself to the potatoes."

> I **cut myself** while I was shaving.
> Did you **enjoy yourself** at the party?
> Sue **taught herself** how to cook.

3. We can use the reflexive pronoun with the preposition *by* when we mean "alone" or "without any help."

> Lillian painted the bathroom **by herself.**
> He sits **by himself** for hours.

4. We do not usually use reflexive pronouns with verbs such as *dress, wash,* and *shave.* But we can use these verbs with a reflexive pronoun if we want to show someone did something unusual or with a lot of effort.

> I got up, **dressed,** and went to work.
> Timmy is only three years old, but he can **dress himself.**

---

6 | Practice

Complete the sentences with the correct reflexive pronoun.

1. A: What a beautiful dress! Where did you buy it?

   B: I made it _____*myself.*_____

2. A: Do you want me to go shopping with you?

   B: No, I prefer to go by _____

3. A: Who painted your house?

   B: We painted it _____

4. A: Could you wash this shirt for me?

B: No, you'll have to wash it _____

5. A: Did Paolo get some help with his homework?

B: No, he did it by _____

6. A: Did Helen buy that birthday cake?

B: No, she made it _____

7. A: Timmy is big for a three-year-old.

B: Yes, and he can dress _____

8. A: Tom and I are going to Min's party.

B: OK. Enjoy _____

9. A: Emily is good with computers.

B: Yes, she taught _____

10. A: Do you want me to turn off the iron?

B: No, it will turn _____ off automatically.

7 | Practice

Johnnie is five and Jenny is seven. They are alone in the kitchen. Complete the sentences with the correct reflexive pronoun.

1. Johnnie and Jenny are trying to make breakfast by ___*themselves.*___

2. Johnnie got the box of cereal from the shelf by _____

3. He helped _____ to the cereal and the milk.

4. He taught _____ how to make cereal when he was four.

5. Jenny was trying to cut a bagel and cut _____

6. Then she tried to toast the bagel and burned _____

7. In the end, Johnnie and Jenny made and ate breakfast by _____

8 | Your Turn

Talk about your family or friends. Say ten things they do themselves. Use *himself, herself, ourselves,* and *themselves.* You may use ideas from the list or your own.

Example:
choose (one's) clothes
My little sister chooses her clothes herself.

choose (one's) clothes	do the laundry	make the bed
clean the windows	fix the car	paint the house
cook the meals	make (one's) clothes	wash the car

5d Another, The Other, Other, Others, and The Others

These cookies are good.
Can I have **another**?

1. We use *another* and *the other* as adjectives before nouns.

	Adjective	Noun
Jenny ate	**another**	cookie.
Melanie ate	**the other**	cookie.

2. We use *another* and *the other* as pronouns.

	Pronoun
Jorge ate	**another.**
Toshi ate	**the other.**

3. We use the adjective *other* (with no –s) with a plural noun.

	Adjective	Noun
There are	**other**	**cookies** in the box.
I like		**kinds** of cookies.

4. We use the pronoun *others* (with –s) when there is no noun that follows.

	Adjective	
There are	**others**	on the plate.

Others = other cookies

1. *Another* means one more of the same thing (or the same group) we had before.

   These cookies are good. Can I have **another?** (one more of the same cookies)

2. *The other* means the one that is left of the same thing.

   There are two pieces of chocolate left. I'll take one and you take **the other.**

3. *Other* and *others* mean several more of the same group. *The others* means the ones left of the same group.

   There are **other** cookies in the box.
   There are **others** in the box.
   These cookies have nuts in them. **The others** have coconut.

9 Practice

Complete the sentences with *another* or *the other*.

1. One country in Europe is France. _Another_ is Italy.

2. There are two countries I want to visit. One is France, and _____ is Italy.

3. Paris is a city in Europe. Rome is _____ city in Europe.

4. In France, people speak French. Belgium is _____ country where people speak French.

5. There are three European countries where people speak French. One is France, _____ is Belgium, and _____ is Switzerland.

6. Paris is a beautiful city in Europe. Prague is _____ beautiful city in Europe.

7. A popular fruit in the United States is the banana. The orange is _____.

8. There are two popular fruits in my home. One is the banana, and _____ is the apple.

9. The potato is a popular vegetable. The carrot is _____.

10. People usually eat three meals. Breakfast is one meal, lunch is _____, and dinner is _____.

11. There are many popular flavors of ice cream. One is vanilla; _____ is strawberry.

12. We buy two flavors of ice cream. One is vanilla, and _____ is chocolate.

10 Practice

Complete the sentences with *other*, *others*, or *the others*.

1. Baseball is a popular sport. _____*Others*_____ are basketball and football.

2. There are three popular team sports at this school. One is baseball. _____ are basketball and football.

3. Some sports are team sports like football. _____, like tennis, are not team sports.

4. There are many kinds of water on the Earth. Oceans are one kind. Some _____ are seas, lakes, and rivers.

5. There are four oceans. The Pacific and the Atlantic are two. _____ are the Indian and the Arctic Oceans.

6. Only one student was late for the test. _____ were on time.

7. Some students live with their parents. _____ live on campus. The rest of the students live in apartments in the city.

8. Some universities give computers to their students. _____ universities don't.

11 Practice

Complete the sentences with *another*, *other*, *the other*, *others*, or *the others*.

1. Our teacher was absent today, so _____ teacher came in her place.

2. I wasn't happy because I like our usual teacher, but all of _____ students in my class were happy.

3. Our usual teacher always gives us homework, but _____ teacher didn't.

4. Some students talk a lot in class. _____ don't, and a few rarely talk.

5. After we finished our exercises in class, she gave us a few _____ to do for homework.

6. Some teachers give a lot of homework. Some _____ teachers don't.

7. A few of us understood the lesson, but some _____ didn't.

8. Some students always ask the teacher questions. All of _____ students keep quiet.

9. There are usually four choices in a multiple choice question. One is correct, and _____ are not correct.

10. Most teachers tell students to write their essays on the computer.

_____ teachers want hand-written essays. Some teachers will accept both.

11. Some teachers give high grades most of the time. Some _____ always give low grades.

12. We have a lot of tests. For example, we have a test today, and we will have _____ test tomorrow.

5e *One* and *Ones*

Man: Do you like the red tie?
Woman: No, I like this **one.**

1. We use the pronoun *one* in the singular and *ones* in the plural so that we do not repeat the noun.

> Do you like the red tie?
> No, I like the blue **one** (tie).
> I never wear brown shoes. I always wear black **ones** (shoes).

2. *One/ones* and *some/any* are indefinite (like the article *a*). *It* and *they/them* refer to something definite (like the article *the*).

> I don't have a passport. I need **one.**
> I don't have any envelopes. I need **some.**

> I have my passport. I received **it** yesterday.
> I have envelopes. I bought **them** yesterday.

12 Practice

Complete the sentences with *one* or *ones*.

1. A: Which is your car?

   B: The black _one_ .

2. A: Can I borrow your dictionary?

   B: Sorry, I don't have _____ .

3. A: I need a ticket.

   B: I have _____ .

4. A: Which phone did you use?

   B: The _____ on your desk.

5. A: I like your shoes.

   B: Oh, thanks. They are the _____ I bought yesterday.

6. A. Which pants fit you better?

   B: The black _____ .

7. A: Hand me the glass, please.

   B: Which _____ ?

8. A: Which scarves do you like best?

   B: The expensive _____ .

13 Practice

Complete the sentences with *one, ones, some, it,* or *them*.

1. I'm sorry, but I broke this glass. I dropped _____ _it._ _____

2. I'm making a sandwich. Would you like _____ , too?

3. If you need change for the parking meter, I have _____

4. She bought some cookies and ate all of _____

5. My computer broke down, so I bought a new _____ this week.

6. Where are my glasses? Do you see _____ .

7. I am throwing away the old magazines and keeping the new _____

8. I bought some greeting cards. I got funny _____ this year.

9. A: Where's your car?

   B: I parked _____ in the parking lot behind the building.

10. I don't have any stamps, but Lin has _____

11. We need to call a taxi. I'll call for _____

12. I don't like the white roses. I prefer the red _____

5f Indefinite Pronouns (*Something, Somebody, Anything, Anybody, Everything, Everybody, Nothing,* and *Nobody*)

This is strange. There's **something** wrong. The door is open.

I don't hear **anything,** and there isn't **anybody** in the house.

	Affirmative Sentences	Negative Sentences	Questions
People	someone/somebody	anyone/anybody	anyone/anybody
	no one/nobody		no one/nobody
	everyone/everybody		everyone/everybody
Things	something	anything	anything/something
	nothing		nothing
	everything		everything
Places	somewhere	anywhere	anywhere/somewhere
	everywhere		everywhere

1. We use *someone/somebody* (a person), *something* (a thing), and *somewhere* (a place) in affirmative statements.

   I can see **somebody** in the store.
   He lives **somewhere** near the airport.

2. We use *anyone/anybody, anything,* and *anywhere* for questions and negative statements.

   I can't hear **anything.**
   Is there **anybody** here?

3. We can use *no one/nobody, nothing,* and *nowhere* in place of *not anyone/anybody, not anything,* and *not anywhere.*

   There isn't **anybody** in the house.
   There is **nobody** in the house.

4. We use the adjective *every* with singular count nouns.

   Every student must take the test. (*Every* student means "all the students.")

5. We use the pronouns *everyone/everybody, everything,* and the adverb *everywhere* in affirmative statements and questions. We use a singular verb with these pronouns.

   Is everybody here?
   Yes, **everybody is** here, but **everything is not** ready for the party.

Function

1. Unlike other pronouns, indefinite pronouns do not take the place of a noun or a noun phrase.

2. We use indefinite pronouns with *some* and *any* to talk about an unknown person, place, or thing.

   I saw **someone** take your jacket. (I don't know who took it.)
   I put my glasses **somewhere,** and now I can't find them.
   (I don't know where I put them.)
   Did you find **anything** to eat? (I don't know if you found some food or not.)

3. We use indefinite pronouns with *every* to talk about all people, places, or things that we are talking about.

   We invited **everyone** to the party.
   Did they go **everywhere** in New York?
   They didn't buy **everything** they wanted.

|14| Practice

Underline the correct word in parentheses.

A.

Ben: I lost my grammar book yesterday. I left it (<u>somewhere</u>/anywhere).
                                                          1

Lee: Did you look in the classroom?

Ben: Yes, I did. It wasn't there. It isn't (everywhere/anywhere).
2

Lee: Did you ask (anyone/nobody)?
3

Ben: Yes, I asked my teacher, and I asked (everyone/anyone) in my class.
4

Lee: Don't worry. You can share a book with (someone/no one) in class tomorrow.
5

Ben: But I don't want to share a book with (anyone/someone). I want my book. I have
6

all the answers in it.

B.

Nancy: I have (nothing/anything) to do this afternoon. Let's go (somewhere/anywhere).
1 2

I have my mother's car so we can go (anywhere/nowhere) we like.
3

Tina: Well, I don't want to go (somewhere/anywhere) special because I'm not wearing
4

dressy clothes.

Nancy: OK. Then, let's get (something/anything) to eat and go (somewhere/anywhere)
5 6

nice and quiet where (nobody/somebody) can disturb us.
7

Tina: That's a great idea. I haven't done (something/anything) like this for a long time.
8

C.

Claudia is going to a party on Saturday, but she has (anything/nothing) to wear.
1

She went to the big department store near her home yesterday but didn't find

(something/anything) nice. This morning she went (somewhere/anywhere) else, but
2 3

(everything/anything) was expensive. At another store, (everything/anything) was nice,
4 5

but (nothing/anything) would fit her. There's (nowhere/everywhere) else to go. Claudia is
6 7

going to look in her closet and find (something/anything) to wear to the party.
8

| 15 | Your Turn |

Work in pairs. Make up six song titles with the pronouns from the list.

Example:
"Everybody Needs Someone to Love"

somewhere   something
someone   anything
nothing   everywhere

WRITING: Write a Personal Description

Write a description of your best friend.

Step 1. Think about your best friend. Write the answers to the following questions. Then think of other things to say about your friend.

1. What is your friend's name?
2. Does your friend have any brothers or sisters?
3. What does your friend do?
4. What does your friend like?
5. What does your friend dislike?
6. What do you do together?
7. Why do you like your friend?

Step 2. Rewrite your answers in paragraph form. Write a title in a few words (My Best Friend). For more writing guidelines, see pages 199–203.

Step 3. Evaluate your paragraph.

Checklist

_____ Did you indent the first line?

_____ Did you give your paragraph a title?

_____ Did you put the title at the top center of the page?

Step 4. Edit your work. Work with a partner to edit your sentences. Correct spelling, punctuation, vocabulary, and grammar.

Step 5. Write your final copy.

SELF-TEST

A **Choose the best answer, A, B, C, or D, to complete the sentence. Mark your answer by darkening the oval with the same letter.**

1. Is this _____ suitcase?

   A. hers   Ⓐ Ⓑ Ⓒ Ⓓ
   B. her
   C. her's
   D. she's

2. Oh no! Our teacher is giving us _____ test this week.

   A. other   Ⓐ Ⓑ Ⓒ Ⓓ
   B. the another
   C. another
   D. another one

3. Sue: I like your shoes.
   Pam: These are _____ I bought in Italy.

   A. the one   Ⓐ Ⓑ Ⓒ Ⓓ
   B. the ones
   C. others
   D. ones

4. There isn't a drugstore _____!

   A. anywhere   Ⓐ Ⓑ Ⓒ Ⓓ
   B. anything
   C. nothing
   D. somewhere

5. I don't have my credit card. I left _____ at the store.

   A. one   Ⓐ Ⓑ Ⓒ Ⓓ
   B. them
   C. it
   D. some

6. I left _____ homework at home.

   A. mine   Ⓐ Ⓑ Ⓒ Ⓓ
   B. my
   C. myself
   D. me

7. The children enjoyed _____ at Disneyland, but their parents didn't.

   A. theirselves   Ⓐ Ⓑ Ⓒ Ⓓ
   B. theyselves
   C. them
   D. themselves

8. There _____ to park on this street.

   A. is anywhere   Ⓐ Ⓑ Ⓒ Ⓓ
   B. isn't somewhere
   C. isn't nowhere
   D. isn't anywhere

9. I need a quarter. Do you have _____?

   A. one   Ⓐ Ⓑ Ⓒ Ⓓ
   B. quarter
   C. it
   D. a

10. That is _____.

    A. ours car   Ⓐ Ⓑ Ⓒ Ⓓ
    B. our car
    C. car ours
    D. ourselves car

B **Find the underlined word or phrase, A, B, C, or D, that is incorrect. Mark your answer by darkening the oval with the same letter.**

1. Some teachers can remember all the
   A   B
   student names.
   C   D

   Ⓐ Ⓑ Ⓒ Ⓓ

2. If you don't like your job, you can look
                        A   B
   for other one.
       C   D

   Ⓐ Ⓑ Ⓒ Ⓓ

3. Nobody mentioned the problem to
   A   B   C
   ourselves.
   D

   Ⓐ Ⓑ Ⓒ Ⓓ

4. We took our little sister with us because
          A   B
   she doesn't like to stay home by ourself.
                                 C   D

   Ⓐ Ⓑ Ⓒ Ⓓ

5. I didn't buy the shirt because I have one
                  A   B
   just like her in another color.
            C   D

   Ⓐ Ⓑ Ⓒ Ⓓ

6. Only two of the questions on the exam
                    A   B
   were easy. Others were difficult.
              C   D

   Ⓐ Ⓑ Ⓒ Ⓓ

7. There are two very popular cities
                              A
   in the United States. One is New York,
            B   C
   and another is San Francisco.
       D

   Ⓐ Ⓑ Ⓒ Ⓓ

8. In a multiple choice question, one of the
                                  A
   choices is correct, and others are incorrect.
   B   C   D

   Ⓐ Ⓑ Ⓒ Ⓓ

9. We looked at my old videos last night,
                 A   B
   and we enjoyed themselves a lot.
                  C   D

   Ⓐ Ⓑ Ⓒ Ⓓ

10. Our friend is in the hospital because he
    A
    burned himself by accident, so we visited
           B   C
    himself last night.
    D

   Ⓐ Ⓑ Ⓒ Ⓓ

128

UNIT 6

THE PERFECT TENSES

6a The Present Perfect Tense

Form

Claudia and Kenny are in New York.
They **have visited** many places.
They **have seen** the Statue of Liberty.
They **have gone** up to the top of the
Empire State Building, and **they've been**
to Central Park.

1. We use the past participle verb form in the present perfect tense. The past participle form of regular verbs is the same as the simple past tense form.

Simple Past Tense Form	Part Participle
washed	**washed**
finished	**finished**

2. The past participle of irregular verbs is often different from the simple past form. See page 196 for a list of irregular verbs.

Simple Past Tense Form	Part Participle
ate	**eaten**
came	**come**
did	**done**
drank	**drunk**
knew	**known**
saw	**seen**
spoke	**spoken**
took	**taken**
was	**been**
went	**gone**

3. We form the present perfect tense with *have* or *has* + the past participle of the verb.

AFFIRMATIVE AND NEGATIVE STATEMENTS		
Subject	*Have/Has (Not)*	Past Participle
I You	**have** **'ve** **have not** **'ve not** **haven't**	
He/She/It	**has** **'s** **has not** **'s not** **hasn't**	**arrived.**
We They	**have** **'ve** **have not** **'ve not** **haven't**	

YES/NO QUESTIONS			SHORT ANSWERS	
Have/Has	Subject	Past Participle	Yes,	No,
Have	I		you **have.**	you **haven't.**
	you		I/we **have.**	I/we **haven't.**
Has	he/she/it	**arrived?**	he/she/it **has.**	he/she/it **hasn't.**
Have	we		you **have.**	you **haven't.**
	they		they **have.**	they **haven't.**

WH- QUESTIONS				
Wh- Word	*Have/Has*	Subject	Past Participle	
Where	**have**	they	**been?**	
What	**have**	you	**made**	for lunch?
Why	**has**	the music	**stopped?**	
Who*	**has**	she	**spoken**	to?
How many (movies)	**have**	we	**seen**	this year?
How long	**have**	you	**been**	ill?

*In formal written English, the wh- word would be *whom*.

The Perfect Tenses

1. We use the present perfect tense for an action or situation that happened at some unspecified time in the past. The exact time is not important. The action or situation has importance in the present.

> They**'ve been** to New York. (We're talking about their experiences as of *now*.)
> I**'ve washed** the car. (It's clean *now*.)
> He **hasn't done** his homework. (We're talking about his situation *now*.)

2. We can also use the present perfect to talk about actions that were repeated in the past. The exact time is not stated or important.

> We**'ve taken** two tests this month.
> I**'ve been** to New York three times.

3. We often use the present perfect with the time expressions *for, since, just, already, yet, recently,* and *how long.*

> Lin **has lived** here **since** 1999.
> I **have known** you **for** three years.

---

1 | Practice

Complete the postcard that Kenny wrote to his friend Brian. Use the present perfect tense of the verbs in parentheses.

Dear Brian,

We (be) _____*have been*_____ in New York
                1

for four days, and we have enjoyed it very much. We

(go) _____ to the Empire State
        2

Building, we (see) _____ the Statue
             3

of Liberty, and we (walk) _____ in
                4

Central Park. We (eat) _____ great
            5

food every day, and we (buy) _____
                6

tickets for a Broadway show. We still (not, visit)

_____ the Metropolitan Museum
       7

of Art, but we are going there tomorrow. Claudia

(come) _____ back from
        8

shopping, so I'll close now.

Kenny

Mr. Brian Shih
4125 E. 25th Rd.
Phoenix, AZ 86000

Practice

Work with a partner. Ask and answer questions with the prompts about what Claudia and Kenny have done in New York. Then write your questions and answers.

1. Claudia and Kenny/arrive in New York

   Have Claudia and Kenny arrived in New York?

   Yes, they have.

2. they/enjoy/New York

   _____

   _____

3. they/go/to the Empire State Building

   _____

   _____

4. they/see/the Statue of Liberty

   _____

   _____

5. they/walk/in Central Park

   _____

   _____

6. they/eat/good food

   _____

   _____

7. they/buy/tickets for a Broadway show

   _____

   _____

8. they/visit/the Metropolitan Museum of Art

   _____

   _____

Practice

Complete the conversation with wh- or yes/no questions in the present perfect.

Sue: I haven't seen Claudia and Kenny all week. Where are they?

Pete: You didn't know? They've gone away on vacation.

Sue: Really! _Where have they gone?_____
                                           1

Pete: They've gone to New York.

Sue: How long _____
                                        2

Pete: They've been in New York for four days now.

Sue: _____
                                        3

Pete: They've seen the Empire State Building, St. Patrick's Cathedral, and Central Park.

Sue: _____ any interesting
                              4

       restaurants?

Pete: Oh, yes. They've eaten in Chinese, Korean, Greek, Brazilian, and Indian restaurants.

Sue: _____
                                        5

Pete: No, but they're going to visit the Metropolitan Museum of Art before they leave.

Practice

Armando's roommate Daniel is a problem. Complete the dialogue with the present perfect of the verbs in parentheses.

Armando: Daniel, I'm sorry, but it's time for you to find another place to live.

Daniel: Why? What's wrong?

Armando: What's wrong? You (be) _____ a terrible roommate.
                                           1

          For example, today you (eat) _____ my food, you
                                                2

          (drink) _____ my milk, and you
                       3

          (break) _____ my CD player.
                       4

Daniel: Don't be so sensitive, Armando. I'll replace those things for you.

Armando: That's not all. You (not, pay) _____ the rent for
                                               5

          two months. You (insult) _____ my sister, and you
                                          6

(try) _____ to steal my girlfriend. I
7

(be) _____ very patient, but now it's time for you to
8

leave.

Daniel: Well, OK. I'll leave if you want. But...

Armando: What?

Daniel: I (spend) _____ all of my money. Could you lend me $500?
9

5 | Practice

Complete the conversation with the present perfect of the verbs in parentheses.

Marco: What things (do) ___*have*___ you ___*done*___ up to now?
                               1   2

Tina: Lots of things. I (wash) _____ the dishes, and I
                                  3

(make) _____ the bed. I (go) _____
      4   5

to the store, and I (buy) _____ groceries. What have
                       6

you done?

Marco: I (take) _____ a shower, I (do) _____
             7   8

my homework, and I (clean) _____ my room. And...oh, yes.
                            9

I (have) _____ lunch.
            10

6 | Practice

Work in pairs. Make a dialogue similar to the one in Practice 5 about yourselves.

Example:
You: What have you done today?
Your partner: I've studied for the test tomorrow, and I've cleaned my room.
You: I haven't studied for the test, but I've done all of my homework.

7 | Your Turn

Think of things to do and places to see in the town where you are now. Make a list of five things to do or places to see. Ask other people what they have done in your town.

Example:
You: Have you been to the cathedral?
Your partner: Yes, I have. Have you been to the zoo?
You: No, I haven't. Have you visited the art museum?

6b *For* and *Since*

This house has been here **since** 1925.
My grandmother has lived here **for** 50 years.

1. We use *for* with the present perfect when we are talking about a period or length of time that started in the past and continues to the present.

   I've lived here **for** three years.

2. We use *since* with the present perfect when we are talking about a point of time in the past such as a date, a month, or a day.

   I've worked here **since** August.
   She's been sick **since** Tuesday.

8 Practice

Some of these time expressions are used with *for*. Others are used with *since*. Put them in the correct list.

2003	I was a child	Monday
a long time	last month	my birthday
about a week	two months	six hours
New Year's Eve	last summer	ten minutes
eight o'clock	30 seconds	three years
Friday evening	many years	yesterday
I moved here	May	

I have been here...	I have been here...
for	**since**
a long time	*2003*

9 Practice

Complete the sentences with *for* or *since*.

1. Rob has had his car _____*for*_____ a year, but he wants to sell it.

2. He's had problems with it _____ the day he bought it.

3. The lights haven't worked _____ March.

4. It has made a funny noise _____ several weeks.

5. He has taken it to a mechanic every week _____ a month.

6. He has spent a lot of money on it every month _____ June.

7. He has run an advertisement in the newspaper every day _____ a week.

8. So far, he hasn't had a response _____ he ran the ad.

10 Your Turn

Work with a partner. Ask questions with *how long* and the prompts. Your partner answers the questions using *for* or *since*.

Example:
be in this country
You: How long have you been in this country?
Your partner: I have been here for eight months.

be in this country   have your watch   live in your apartment   study in this class

6c *Ever* and *Never*

A: Have you **ever** seen the Taj Mahal?
B: No, **never.**

1. We can use *ever* in questions, often with the present perfect. It means "at any time up to now."

2. When we use *ever* in present perfect tense questions, it comes between the subject and the past participle.

   Have you **ever** been to China?

3. We often use *never* (at no time) when we give a negative answer.

   No, I've **never** been to China.

|II| Practice

Interview the famous movie star La La Labore. Write questions with the prompts and give short answers.

1. ever be/married

   _Have you ever been married?_____

   Yes, _____*I have.*_____ I've been married eight times.

2. ever be/to Hollywood

   _____

   Yes, _____ I've been there many times.

3. ever drive/a Ferrari

_____

No, _____ I never drive. I have a chauffeur.

4. ever give/an interview on television

_____

Yes, _____ I've given interviews to famous journalists.

5. ever write/a book

_____

No, _____ Other people write about me.

6. ever sing/in a movie

_____

No, _____ I can't sing.

7. ever eat/caviar

_____

Yes, _____ I eat it for breakfast every day!

12 Practice

Work with a partner. Ask questions with _have you ever_ and the prompts.

Example:
fly in a helicopter
You: Have you ever flown in a helicopter?
Your partner: Yes, I have. OR No, I never have. OR No, never.

1. fly in a helicopter

2. drive a truck

3. eat Thai food

4. go to Hawaii

5. have the flu

6. hold a snake

7. meet a millionaire

8. play baseball

9. sleep in a tent

10. speak to a famous person

11. swim in a river

12. take a photo of a lion

13. tell a lie

14. travel by boat

6d *Already, Yet, and Just*

They've **just** gotten married.
They've **already** had a ceremony.
They haven't gone on their honeymoon
yet.

1. We use *yet* in negative sentences to say that something has not happened, but we think it will. *Yet* comes at the end of the sentence.

   The plane hasn't arrived **yet.**

2. We also use *yet* in questions to ask if something we expect to happen has happened.

   Has the plane arrived **yet?**

3. We use *just* if the action is very recent. *Just* comes before the past participle.

   I've **just** spoken to Tony.

4. We use *already* to say something happened before now or before it was expected to happen. *Already* comes before the past participle.

   I've **already** told you how to get there.

---

13 Practice

A. **Carlos and Rosa are in San Francisco on vacation. It's their last day. Read this list of things they want to do today. They have done some of these things, but they haven't done others yet. A check mark (√) shows what they have already done.**

1. √ get postcards
2. write postcards
3. have lunch
4. √ visit the Museum of Modern Art
5. √ see a show

6. buy souvenirs
7. ask the hotel for the bill
8. √ pack the suitcases
9. go to the post office
10. call the airline

B. Write sentences with *already* and *yet*.

1. *They've already gotten postcards.*
2. *They haven't written postcards yet.*
3. _____
4. _____
5. _____
6. _____
7. _____
8. _____
9. _____
10. _____

14 Your Turn

Write five sentences about things you've recently done and things you haven't done yet this week.

Example:
I've just paid the bills.
I've already done my homework.
I haven't called my mother yet.

1. _____
    _____
2. _____
    _____
3. _____
    _____
4. _____
    _____
5. _____
    _____

15 Your Turn

Work with a partner. Read each other's sentences from Practice 14. Ask and answer questions about what you've done and haven't done.

Example:
You: Have you paid the bills yet?
Your partner: Yes, I have.

6e   The Simple Past Tense OR The Present Perfect Tense

Antonia Beck **has been** to Turkey.
She **went** there in 2001.

1. We use the simple past tense when we are talking about the past. We use it for actions that happened in the past. We can state the specific time of the action.

   She **went** to Turkey in July, 2001. After a month, she **went** to Athens.

2. We use the present perfect for an action that happened in the past. The action has importance in the present. The specific time is unimportant, and we cannot state it.

   CORRECT: Antonia **has been** to Turkey.
   INCORRECT: Antonia has been to Turkey ~~in 2001.~~

3. We use the simple past for an action that started and finished in the past.

   George **had** a headache for two hours this morning. (He doesn't have a headache now.)

4. We use the present perfect for an action that started in the past and is still continuing in the present.

   George **has had** a headache for two hours. (He still has a headache.)

16 Practice

Complete the sentences with the simple past or present perfect of the verbs in parentheses.

1. A: I (see) _____*saw*_____ Karen yesterday.

   B: Oh really? I (not/see) _____ her for weeks.

2. A: What (do) _____ you _____ last Saturday?

B: I (stay) _____ at home.

3. A: (write) _____ you _____ your essay yet?

B: Yes, I (finish) _____ it an hour ago.

4. A: (be) _____ you _____ to the United States?

B: Yes, I (go) _____ to Miami last summer.

5. A: I (know) _____ Tony for three years.

B: Really? When (meet) _____ you _____ him?

A: We (meet) _____ in college.

6. A: (eat) _____ you _____ at Mario's restaurant?

B: Yes, I _____. I (eat) _____ there last Saturday.

7. A: (ever, play) _____ you _____ _____ soccer?

B: Yes, I (play) _____ when I was a teenager.

8. A: (ask) _____ you _____ the teacher about your essay yet?

B: Yes, I (talk) _____ to her yesterday.

|17| Practice

Antonia Beck has made a lot of business trips in the last few years. Say which cities she has visited. Then say when she went there. Use the simple past and the present perfect.

Example:
She has been to New York.
She went there in May, 2001.

2001		**2003**	
May	New York	February	Boston
September	Bangkok	April	Mexico City
December	Paris	October	Istanbul
2002		**2004**	
March	Tokyo	January	Cairo
July	Chicago	July	Jakarta
September	Seoul	September	Rio de Janeiro

6f   The Present Perfect Progressive Tense

Tony **has been waiting** for 45 minutes.

We form the present perfect progressive tense with *have/has* + the past participle of *be* (*been*) + verb + *-ing*.

AFFIRMATIVE AND NEGATIVE STATEMENTS			
Subject	*Have/Has (Not)*	*Been*	Verb + *-ing*
I	**have** **'ve**	**been**	**waiting.**
You	**have not** **'ve not** **haven't**		
He/She/It	**has** **'s** **has not** **'s not** **hasn't**		
We	**have** **'ve**		
They	**have not** **'ve not** **haven't**		

YES/NO QUESTIONS				SHORT ANSWERS	
Have/Has	Subject	*Been*	Verb + *-ing*	Yes,	No,
Have	I	**been**	**waiting?**	you **have.**	you **haven't.**
	you			I/we **have.**	I/we **haven't.**
Has	he/she/it			he/she/it **has.**	he/she/it **hasn't.**
Have	we			you **have.**	you **haven't.**
	they			they **have.**	they **haven't.**

We use the present perfect progressive to talk about an action that began in the past and continues into the present. We can use this tense to show how long an activity has been in progress. We use the time words *for* and *since* for this.

> He **has been waiting for** 45 minutes.
> She **has been talking** on the phone **since** six o'clock.

18 Practice

Complete the sentences with the present progressive or present perfect progressive of the verbs in parentheses.

A.

A: Who (wait) ___*are*___ you ___*waiting*___ for?
                   1   2

B: I (wait) _____ for the manager.
                3

A: She (talk) _____ on the phone with a client for an hour. I'll tell
              4

you when she's free.

B.

A: You look busy. What (do) _____ you _____?
               1   2

B: I (write) _____ my research paper.
             3

A: How long (work) _____ you _____ on it?
               4   5

B: I (work) _____ on it since January.
             6

C.

At the moment, I (sit) _____ in class. I (sit) _____
                    1   2

here for 20 minutes. We (learn) _____ about the present perfect
                       3

progressive tense since the beginning of this class.

19 Practice

Write answers using the present perfect progressive and a time expression with *for* or *since*.

1. How long have you been going to this school?

   I have been going to this school since September.

2. How long have you been learning English?

_____

3. How long have you been using this book?

_____

4. How long have you been sitting in this classroom today?

_____

5. How long have you been learning the present perfect tense?

_____

6. How long have you been doing this exercise?

_____

20 Your Turn

Work with a partner. Ask and answer questions about your lives with *how long* + the present perfect progressive. Use the list of verbs for ideas.

Example:
You: How long have you been living in your house?
Your partner: I've been living there for six months.

live   stay   study   work

6g The Present Perfect Tense OR The Present Perfect Progressive Tense

Karen **has been talking** on the phone for two hours.
She **has made** four telephone calls.

1. We use the present perfect for an action that has just finished or that was finished at some unstated point in the past.

   > He **has just missed** the bus.
   > I **have missed** the bus, but I won't be late.

2. We use the present perfect progressive for an action that started in the past and continues into the present.

   > Mr. Black **has been teaching** for nine years.

3. We use the present perfect to talk about a repeated action.

   > She **has made** four telephone calls.

4. We use the present perfect progressive to emphasize the duration of the action.

   > She **has been talking** on the phone for two hours.

5. With some verbs that take place over time, like *live, stay, study, teach,* and *work,* we can use either the present perfect or the present perfect progressive.

   > He **has been teaching** for nine years.
   > OR He **has taught** for nine years.

21 Practice

Complete the sentences with the present perfect or the present perfect progressive of the verbs in parentheses.

1. Carlos and Rosa are planning to buy a house. They

   (look) _have been looking_ for a house for a month. They

   (look) _____ at five houses, but they

   (not, find) _____ one that they like yet.

2. My grandfather (paint) _____ for ten years now. He

   (paint) _____ more than fifty paintings.

3. I (learn) _____ to drive for four months. I

   (take) _____ the driving test three times now and

   (not, pass) _____ yet.

4. John (write) _____ on his computer for an hour. He

   (already, send) _____ five e-mail messages to his friends.

5. Karen (drive) _____ for three hours now. She

   (drive) _____ almost 200 miles.

6. I (read) _____ this book for two weeks now, but I

(not, finish) _____ yet.

7. Jerry (work) _____ on a math problem for half an hour,

and he (not, find) _____ the answer yet.

8. I (cook) _____ for hours, and I

(just, burn) _____ the cake.

22 Practice

Complete the sentences with the present perfect or the present perfect progressive of the verbs in parentheses.

Dear Sarah,

    I (mean) _____*have been meaning*_____ to write to you for weeks,
                    1

but you know how it is. Everything is fine here at home. I (just, finish)

_____ my second year at college, and I (get)
        2

_____ good grades. I (decide)
        3

_____ to get a job for the summer and save some
        4

money. So far, I (help) _____ Mom with the shopping
                  5

and the cooking.

    Dad (sell) _____ the old car! He (buy)
                  6

_____ a new one of the same make and color, of course! I
        7

(not/drive) _____ it yet. Mom is busy with redecorating the
        8

house. It (be) _____ a mess here. The painters (work)
        9

_____ as fast as they can, and I hope they will be done
        10

soon. The house will look great by the time you come.

    I hope you (study) _____ hard!
               11

    See you soon.

Your brother,

Tim

6h   The Past Perfect Tense

Candice was sad because her friends **hadn't asked** her to go biking with them.

We form the past perfect tense with *had* + the past participle of the verb.

AFFIRMATIVE AND NEGATIVE STATEMENTS		
Subject	*Had (Not)*	Past Participle
I	**had**	
You	**'d**	
He/She/It		**left.**
We	**had not**	
They	**hadn't**	

YES/NO QUESTIONS			SHORT ANSWERS	
Had	Subject	Past Participle	Yes,	No,
Had	I	**left?**	you **had.**	you **hadn't.**
	you		I/we **had.**	I/we **hadn't.**
	he/she/it		he/she/it **had.**	he/she/it **hadn't.**
	we		you **had.**	you **hadn't.**
	they		they **had.**	they **hadn't.**

1. We use the past perfect for a past action that happened before another past action.

2. We use the past perfect for the first action in time, and the simple past for the second action.

1st Action   **2nd Action**

When he **had saved** enough money, he **bought** a car.

3. The past perfect verb can come after the simple past verb. The verb tenses tell you which action happened first.

2nd Action   **1st Action**

He **bought** a car when he **had saved** enough money.

23 Practice

Complete the sentences with the simple past or past perfect of the verbs in parentheses.

A.

When I (get) _____*got*_____ home yesterday, the letter

(arrive) _____. I (open) _____ it
           2   3

and (read) _____ it. It said that they
           4

(give) _____ the position to someone else because that person
         5

(have) _____ more experience.
         6

B.

When I (get) _____ home, my son
         1

(eat, already) _____ dinner. He said he was hungry because he
         2

(not, eat) _____ all day. Then, he (get) _____
         3   4

sick because he (eat) _____ too much ice cream.
         5

Ken's mother and father-in-law are coming to stay for a few days. Look at the things Ken and his wife did and didn't do before their guests arrived. Write sentences using the past perfect tense.

1. They changed the sheets.
2. They bought food.
3. They developed the photographs of their daughter.
4. They didn't prepare dinner.
5. They didn't rent any interesting movies.
6. They didn't do the laundry.
7. They washed the dishes.
8. They didn't clean the house.

Ken's mother and father-in-law arrived on Friday at 5:00 P.M. By that time,

1. _Ken and his wife had changed the sheets._

2. _By that time,_

3. _By that time,_

4. _By that time,_

5. _By that time,_

6. _By that time,_

7. _By that time,_

8. _By that time,_

25 Practice

Work with a partner. Give two possible answers for each of these questions. Give one in the simple past and the other in the past perfect. Then write your answers. Use the ideas from the list or your own.

be unhappy	get a better offer	not bring/his wallet	study the night before
feel sick	her car/be stolen	not like/the menu	the neighbors/be loud

1. Why did he fail the test?

  He failed the test because he felt sick during the test.

  He failed the test because he had not studied the night before.

2. Why did he leave his job?

  _____

  _____

3. Why did he leave the restaurant?

  _____

  _____

4. Why did she call the police?

  _____

  _____

26 Your Turn

Think of a point in your life when your life changed, such as:

1. you turned sixteen
2. you got your first car
3. you started/left school
4. you got married
5. the year 20XX

Write three things you had done before then.
Write three things that you hadn't done before then.

Example:
Before I turned sixteen, I hadn't driven a car.

6i The Past Perfect Progressive Tense

Bob Blake was hot and nervous.
He **had been sitting** in a meeting
with his boss for two hours.

We form the past perfect progressive tense with *had been* + verb + *–ing*.

AFFIRMATIVE AND NEGATIVE STATEMENTS		
Subject	*Had (Not)*	*Been + Verb + -ing*
I	**had**	
You	**'d**	
He/She/It		**been working.**
We	**had not**	
They	**hadn't**	

YES/NO QUESTIONS			SHORT ANSWERS	
Had	Subject	*Been + Verb + -ing*	Yes,	No,
Had	I	**been working?**	you **had.**	you **hadn't.**
	you		I/we **had.**	I/we **hadn't.**
	he/she/it		he/she/it **had.**	he/she/it **hadn't.**
	we		you **had.**	you **hadn't.**
	they		they **had.**	they **hadn't.**

1. We use the past perfect progressive as the past of the present perfect progressive.

2. The past perfect progressive emphasizes the duration of an action that started and finished in the past.

Past Perfect Progressive Tense	Present Perfect Progressive Tense
He **had been waiting** for me for an hour. (He isn't waiting now.)	He **has been waiting** for me for an hour. (He is still waiting now.)

3. We also use the past perfect progressive to show the cause of an action that happened in the past.

Result   **Cause**
Her eyes were tired. She **had been working** on the computer for hours.

27 Practice

What had they been doing? Complete the sentences using the verbs from the list and the past perfect progressive.

dream   lie   run   try   walk   wait

1. Sophie's feet ached. She ___*had been walking*___ in her new shoes for hours.

2. Louis was angry. He _____ for Kim for 45 minutes.

3. Carmen woke up at 3:00 in the morning. She was frightened. She

   _____.

4. Ted was hot and out of breath when he came in. He _____

   in the park.

5. Tony came in from the beach looking very red. He _____

   in the sun too long.

6. The students were confused. They _____ to learn the past

   perfect progressive.

28 Your Turn

When was the last time: • you were tired   • you were angry   • you were nervous

What had you been doing? How long had you been doing it? Tell your partner.

Example:
The last time I was tired was on Saturday. I had been cleaning the apartment all day.

Write a letter to a friend about your recent experiences.

Step 1. Think about things in your past and present life you can write about. Write the answers to these questions or others you can think of.

1. What are you studying?

_____

2. How long have you been studying?

_____

3. What do you find easy/difficult/interesting?

_____

4. What have you been doing in your free time?

_____

5. Where is the last place you traveled to? What did you do there?

_____

6. What movies have you seen? What kind of sports have you been doing or have you watched on television?

_____

7. What special things have you bought?

_____

8. When will you talk to your friend again, or maybe see your friend?

_____

Step 2. Rewrite the answers in the form of a letter. For more writing guidelines, see pages 407–411.

Step 3. Evaluate your letter.

Checklist

_____ Did you include the date at the top of the letter?

_____ Did you start with a greeting such as "Dear Rosa"?

_____ Did you indent your paragraphs?

_____ Did you end with a closing such as "Sincerely," "Your friend," or "Love"?

_____ Did you sign your name at the bottom of your letter?

Step 4. Edit your letter. Work with a partner or teacher to edit your sentences. Correct spelling, punctuation, vocabulary, and grammar.

Step 5. Write the final copy of your letter.

SELF-TEST

A Choose the best answer, A, B, C, or D, to complete the sentence. Mark your answer by darkening the oval with the same letter.

1. I _____ since 10:00 when the doorbell rang.

   A. was sleeping   Ⓐ Ⓑ Ⓒ Ⓓ
   B. have been sleeping
   C. slept
   D. had been sleeping

2. Sandy _____ a new computer last week. She likes it.

   A. bought   Ⓐ Ⓑ Ⓒ Ⓓ
   B. had bought
   C. was buying
   D. had been bought

3. Sam has lived in San Francisco _____ three years.

   A. since   Ⓐ Ⓑ Ⓒ Ⓓ
   B. for
   C. already
   D. yet

4. She _____.

   A. is just arrived   Ⓐ Ⓑ Ⓒ Ⓓ
   B. just arrive
   C. has just arrived
   D. arrived just

5. I _____ my homework.

   A. have done already   Ⓐ Ⓑ Ⓒ Ⓓ
   B. did already
   C. have already done
   D. arrived just

6. I _____.

   A. haven't finished yet   Ⓐ Ⓑ Ⓒ Ⓓ
   B. didn't finish yet
   C. haven't yet finished
   D. didn't yet finish

7. After he _____, he called a taxi.

   A. has packed   Ⓐ Ⓑ Ⓒ Ⓓ
   B. was packing
   C. pack
   D. had packed

8. I _____ such a strange story in my life.

   A. never heard   Ⓐ Ⓑ Ⓒ Ⓓ
   B. have never heard
   C. heard never
   D. have heard never

9. I _____ you since December.

   A. haven't saw   Ⓐ Ⓑ Ⓒ Ⓓ
   B. haven't seen
   C. didn't see
   D. not see

10. We _____ our trip to Thailand for a month. We have almost finished, and we are leaving next week.

   A. are planning   Ⓐ Ⓑ Ⓒ Ⓓ
   B. planned
   C. have been planning
   D. had planned

B Find the underlined word or phrase, A, B, C, or D, that is incorrect. Mark your answer by darkening the oval with the same letter.

1. <u>Have</u> you <u>yet</u> learned <u>all</u> <u>the</u> irregular past
     A   B   C D
participles?

2. <u>Have</u> you <u>study</u> English verb tenses <u>when</u>
     A   B   C
you <u>were</u> in high school?
     D

3. We <u>have been</u> <u>studying</u> the past tenses <u>for</u>
        A   B   C
the beginning of the <u>semester</u>.
                   D

4. Picasso <u>has painted</u> hundreds of paintings
          A
<u>before</u> he <u>died</u> <u>in</u> 1973.
 B   C D

A B C D

5. My friend <u>had</u> not <u>been</u> <u>working</u> <u>since</u> the
          A   B   C   D
company closed down two months ago.

A B C D

6. <u>The</u> Science Museum <u>had</u> <u>been</u> closed <u>for</u>
   A   B   C   D
five days because of repairs, but it will
open again next Monday.

A B C D

7. <u>Have</u> you <u>seen ever</u> <u>the</u> Statue of Liberty
   A   B   C
<u>in New York</u>?
   D

A B C D

8. <u>How many</u> verb <u>tenses</u> <u>did</u> you <u>studied</u> up
     A   B   C   D
to now?

A B C D

9. <u>Have</u> you <u>see</u> <u>a kangaroo</u> when you <u>were</u>
   A   B   C   D
in Australia last winter?

10. <u>Have</u> you <u>been</u> to London before you <u>were</u>
    A   B   C
there <u>last month</u>?
     D

UNIT 7

QUESTIONS AND PHRASAL VERBS

7a Yes/No Questions and Short Answers

A: Does he fight fires?
B: Yes, he does.

1. When forms of the verbs *be, have,* and *do* are used with other verb forms such as the base form, the *–ing* form, or the past participle, they are auxiliary verbs.

   He **is wearing** a firefighter's uniform. (*Is* is an auxiliary verb.)
   Does he **fight** fires? (*Does* is an auxiliary verb.)
   He **has fought** many fires. (*Has* is an auxiliary verb.)

2. Modal verbs such as *can, should,* and *will* are also auxiliary verbs.

   He **should** be careful on the job!

3. Auxiliary verbs are used to form tenses, questions, and negative statements.

4. There are 17 common auxiliary verbs in English that we use to make questions. Auxiliary verbs are also used to make short answers.

YES/NO QUESTIONS				SHORT ANSWERS	
Auxilary Verb	Subject	Base Verb or Base Verb + *-ing* or Past Participle		Yes,	No,
Am	I	**disturbing**	you?	you **are.**	you **aren't.**
Is	it	**raining**	hard?	it **is.**	it **isn't.**
Are	they	**studying**	English?	they **are.**	they **aren't.**
Was	she	**studying**	English last year?	she **was.**	she **wasn't.**
Were	you	**trying**	to call me?	I **was.**	I **wasn't.**
Do	they	**like**	country music?	they **do.**	they **don't.**
Does	this school	**have**	a language lab?	it **does.**	it **doesn't.**
Did	it	**rain**	last night?	it **did.**	it **didn't.**
Have	they	**finished**	their work?	they **have.**	they **haven't.**
Has	Anne	**come**	home yet?	she **has.**	she **hasn't.**
Had	they	**eaten**	yet?	they **had.**	they **hadn't.**
Can	you	**swim**	well?	I **can.**	I **can't.**
Could	you	**ride**	a bike as a child?	I **could.**	I **couldn't.**
Will	they	**be**	here on time?	they **will.**	they **won't.**
Would	you	**go**	outside in a storm?	I **would.**	I **wouldn't.**
Should	you	**see**	a doctor?	I **should.**	I **shouldn't.**
Must	we	**stand**	in this line?	we **must.**	*

*In this meaning, the negative short answer with *must* is "No, we don't have to."

---

1 Practice

Match the questions with the short answers.

_*h*_ **1.** Have you had lunch yet?

_____ **2.** Do you work in the city?

_____ **3.** Is it raining outside?

_____ **4.** Did you take the test yesterday?

_____ **5.** Can I borrow your car?

_____ **6.** Was the test difficult?

_____ **7.** Are your parents coming?

_____ **8.** Must I go with you?

a. Yes, it is.

b. No, you can't.

c. Yes, I do.

d. No, they aren't.

e. No, it wasn't.

f. No, I didn't.

g. Yes, you must.

h. Yes, I have.

2 Practice

Write short answers to these questions.

1. Is New York City the capital of the United States?

   No, it isn't.

2. Was Elvis Presley a scientist?

   No, _____

3. Do they speak English in Australia?

   Yes, _____

4. Did Edison invent the computer?

   No, _____

5. Was Cleopatra Italian?

   No, _____

6. Does rice grow in China?

   Yes, _____

7. Can monkeys climb trees?

   Yes, _____

8. Are there pyramids in Turkey?

   Yes, _____

9. Were there cars 200 years ago?

   No, _____

10. Have humans been to the planet Jupiter?

    No, _____

3 Practice

What kind of person are you? Complete the questions with the correct auxiliary verb. Then answer by checking Yes or No.

1. _Are_ you shy?   _____ Yes _____ No

2. _____ you like sports?   _____ Yes _____ No

3. _____ you worry a lot?   _____ Yes _____ No

4. _____ you get up early?   _____ Yes _____ No

5. _____ you lazy?   _____ Yes _____ No

6. _____ you clean and tidy?   _____ Yes _____ No

7. _____ you cry when you watch a sad movie? _____ Yes _____ No

8. _____ you get angry quickly?   _____ Yes _____ No

9.	_____ friends very important to you?	_____ Yes _____ No
10.	_____ you like to have fun a lot?	_____ Yes _____ No
11.	_____ clothes important to you?	_____ Yes _____ No

4 Your Turn

Ask your partner five yes/no questions. Use your own ideas or the ones in the list.

Example:
friends
You: Do you have a lot of friends?
Your partner: Yes, I do.

friends	music	school	sports

7b Questions with Wh- Words (*What, When, Where, Who(m), Why,* and *How*)

A: **Where** do polar bears live?
B: They live in the Arctic.

A: **What** do they eat?
B: They eat seals and fish.

A: **When** do they have young?
B: In the spring.

1. We call words that start questions "wh- words" because most of them start with the letters *wh*.

2. When the verb in a question is the simple present or past tense of *be* (*am, is, are, was,* or *were*), we make questions by putting the verb before the subject.

Wh- Word	Present or Past of *Be*	Subject
Who	**is**	**she?**
Where	**are**	**those students?**
Why	**were**	**you** late?

3. For questions with all other verbs and tenses, we put an auxiliary verb before the subject.* The verb can be a base verb, an *-ing* verb, or a past participle.

Wh– Word	Auxiliary Verb	Subject	Verb
Where	**have**	**you**	lived?
When	**does**	**she**	arrive?
What	**did**	**he**	do?
Why	**are**	**they**	leaving?
Who**	**can**	**you**	see?
How	**did**	**your team**	win?

*When *who* or *what* is the subject of the question, we do not change the word order. See section 7c on page 166.

**In formal written English, the wh- word would be *whom*.

Function

We use wh- words to ask for information about something.

1. We use *who(m)* * to ask about a person.

| **Who(m)** were you calling? | I was calling Jill. |
| **Who** took my dictionary? | Tom took your dictionary. |

2. We use *what* to ask about a thing.

| **What** is she studying? | She's studying engineering. |

3. We use *when* to ask about dates and times.

| **When** is the test? | It's on Monday at 9:00 A.M. |

4. We use *where* to ask about places.

| **Where** do you live? | I live on Lemon Street. |

5. We use *why* to ask for reasons.

| **Why** are you leaving? | I have to catch a train. |

*In formal written English, *whom* is the object form of *who*. We usually use *who* for both subjects and objects in speech and informal writing.

Who is the person? Read the answers and write questions with the words in parentheses. Then say who the person is.

A.

1. Question: _When was she born?_

 Answer: She was born in 1929. (when)

2. Question: _____

 Answer: She was born in Philadelphia, Pennsylvania. (where)

3. Question: _____

 Answer: She married a prince. (who)

4. Question: _____

 Answer: She lived in Monaco. (where)

5. Question: _____

 Answer: She was famous for her fashionable clothes and her caring for people. (what)

6. Question: _____

 Answer: She died in a car accident in 1982. (when)

The person is _____

B.

1. Question: _____

 Answer: He was born in 1975. (when)

2. Question: _____

 Answer: He was born in Florida, in the United States. (where)

3. Question: _____

 Answer: He studied at Stanford University in California. (where)

4. Question: _____

 Answer: He started to play golf when he was three. (what)

5. Question: _____

 Answer: He became a professional in 1996. (when)

6. Question: _____

 Answer: He is famous because he is already one of the best players of all time, even though he is young. (why)

The person is _____

6 | Your Turn

Write a quiz about your country. Write five questions with *what, when, where, who,* and *why.* Ask the questions to the class.

Example:
What is the name of the lake in the north?
Where do most people live?

1. _____

2. _____

3. _____

4. _____

5. _____

7c Questions with *Who* and *What* as the Subject

Form

What happened?
A man slipped on a banana peel.

Who was it?
It was my boss.

When *who* or *what* is the subject of a question, the word order is the same as in statements. If *who(m)* or *what* is the object of the question, the word order is in the question form.

Who/What as Subject	*Who(m)/What* as Object
Who met you?	Who(m) did you meet?
What happened?	What did you see?

7 Practice

Write questions with *who* or *what*. The underlined word is the answer.

1. Pete saw <u>Karen</u> at the store yesterday.

   Who did Pete see at the store yesterday?

2. <u>Pete</u> saw Karen at the store yesterday.

   _____

3. Karen was buying <u>fresh strawberries</u>.

   _____

4. <u>Karen</u> was buying fresh strawberries.

   _____

5. <u>Karen</u> invited a friend for dinner yesterday.

   _____

6. Karen invited <u>a friend</u> for dinner yesterday.

   _____

8 Practice

A. Read this story about an accident.

There was an accident this morning. It was 10:00, and it was raining. Bob saw a woman jogger crossing the street. Then he heard a loud bang. A white truck had suddenly stopped, and a red car had crashed into the back of the truck. Bob called 911 for the police and an ambulance. At about 10:15, the police and ambulance came. A police officer asked him questions.

B. Complete the questions about the story with *who* or *what*.

1. _Who_ saw the accident?

2. _____ caused the accident? The rain or the jogger?

3. _____ called 911?

4. _____ made the loud bang?

5. _____ happened to the driver of the white truck?

6. _____ happened to the jogger?

7. _____ happened to the driver of the red car?

8. _____ came at 10:15?

9. _____ asked questions?

10. _____ answered questions?

C. With a partner, ask and answer the questions in part B. Use information from the story when possible. If not, use your imagination.

Example:

You: Who saw the accident?
Your partner: Bob saw it.

7d Questions with *Which* and *What*

Which woman has long curly hair?
Which woman has straight hair?

1. We use *what* or *which* to ask about people, places, and things.

2. We use *what* when the choices are not limited.

> **What** sports do you like?
> **What** authors do you like?

3. We use *which* when the choices are limited.

> **Which** is your favorite, swimming or tennis?
> **Which** author do you prefer, Agatha Christie or Steven King?

4. When using *which,* we can say *which, which* + a noun, or *which one.*

> **Which** do you prefer, Christie or King?
> **Which author** do you prefer, Christie or King?
> **Which one** do you prefer, Christie or King?

5. We can use *which* with singular or plural nouns.

> **Which places** did you visit?
> **Which place** was your favorite?

9 | Practice

Complete the questions with *what* or *which*.

Nina: _Which_ countries did you visit in Europe?
         1

Claudia: I went to France and Italy.

Nina: _____ did you like better?
              2

Claudia: I loved France.

Nina: _____ did you buy?
              3

Claudia: I bought some clothes and perfume.

Nina: _____ country had the best clothes: France or Italy?
              4

Claudia: Italy had the best clothes.

Nina: _____ one had the most perfumes?
              5

Claudia: France had the most perfumes. Tourists buy them tax free.

Claudia: I have an Italian scarf for you, but you can choose the color.

         _____ one do you like—the red or the cream color?
              6

Nina: The red one. Thank you.

Nina: _____ French cities did you visit?
         7

Claudia: I went to Paris, Lyon, Nice, and Cannes.

Nina: _____ city was the most beautiful?
         8

Claudia: Paris, of course.

Nina: _____ is a good time to visit Paris?
         9

Claudia: Anytime is good. I prefer spring.

Nina: _____ month, April or May?
         10

Claudia: I prefer May; it's warmer.

Nina: _____ country was cheaper, France or Italy?
         11

Claudia: They are about the same. My company paid for the trip—it was for business,

you see.

10 Practice

Work with a partner. Look at the photo of the two women on page 168.

Ask and answer questions with *which* or *what* about the women. Use the words in the list or your own ideas. You can answer like this:
The one on the right/left.
Neither one.
Both of them.

Example:
You: Which woman has curly hair?
Your partner: The one on the left.

curly hair
dark hair
glasses
laughing
a short-sleeved shirt
smiling
straight hair

7e   Questions with *How*

How long is the blue whale?
It's about 100 feet long.

How much does it weigh?
It weighs more than 2,300 people.

How big is its mouth?
Its mouth can be 20 feet long.

1. We can use *how* alone, without a word such as *much* or *many*.

Use	Example
We use *how* to ask about the way someone is or the way someone does something.	**How** did she sing? She sang beautifully. **How** do I look? You look very handsome. **How** do you change a flat tire? It isn't difficult. I'll show you.
We use *how* to ask about a means of transportation.	**How** did you get here? By plane./I flew. By car./I drove. By train./I took the train. By bus./I took a bus. On foot./I walked.

2. We can use *how* with an adjective or an adverb.

Use	Example
We use *how* + adjective/adverb to ask about qualities of things or how things are done.	**How old** are you? I'm 22. **How tall** is he? He's five feet eight. **How big** is it? It's three feet across. **How quickly** can you come? In five minutes. **How well** did he do on the test? Pretty well. He got a B. **How fast** was she driving? Not very fast. Just 30 miles an hour.

Use	Example

We use *how often* to ask about the frequency that something happens.	**How often** do you have English class?
	  I have class three times a week.
	How often do you go to the gym?
	  I usually go every day.

We can also say *how many times a day/week/month/year* to ask about frequency.	**How many times a week** do you have English class?
	  I have class three times a week.
	How many times a month do you go to the movies?
	  I go once or twice a month.

We use *how much* and *how many* to ask about the amount of something.	

We use *how much* with noncount nouns.	**How much** money do you need?
	  I need a lot of money.
	How much time do we have?
	  Not much.

We use *how many* with count nouns.	**How many** questions are there on the test?
	  50.
	How many sisters and brothers do you have?
	  Just one sister.

We use *how far* to ask about the distance from one place to another.	**How far** is this school from your house?
	  It's about ten blocks.
	How far is New York from Los Angeles?
	  About 3,000 miles.

We use *how long* to ask about a period of time.	**How long** have you been waiting?
	  Not long. Just a few minutes.
	How long did you stay in Houston?
	  We stayed for one week.

We often ask and answer a question about length of time with *it takes* + time.	How long **does it take** to fly there?
	  It takes about six hours.
	How long **did it take** to write this essay?
	  It took about three hours.
	How long **will it take** for the rice to cook?
	  It will take about 20 minutes.

We can also say *how many minutes/ hours/days/weeks/months/years* to ask about length of time.	**How many years** is this passport good for? Ten years.

3. We use *how about* to suggest something. We often use it in response to a statement or question.

Statement or Question	*How About*	Noun/Pronoun/Gerund*
I don't know what to make for dinner.		**spaghetti?**
What would you like to do tonight?	**How about**	**going** to a movie?
I need someone to go to the party with me.		**me?**
We're cleaning the apartment.		**giving** us some help?

*A gerund is a verb + *-ing* that is used as a noun.

What about means the same thing as *how about*.

What about going to a movie?   OR   **How about** going to a movie?

II Practice

Complete the questions about whales with *how, how big, how many/much, how fast, how long,* or *how often.*

1. _How_____ does a whale breathe?

   It blows water high into the air and takes in fresh air.

2. _____ does it come to the surface to breathe?

   It comes to the surface every 15 minutes.

3. _____ is the blue whale's heart?

   Its heart is the size of a small car.

4. _____ kinds of whales are there?

   There are about 80 different kinds of whales.

5. _____ does it live?

   It lives for about 80 years.

6. _____ can it swim?

   It can swim 30 miles an hour.

7. _____ blue whales are there?

   There are about 5,000 blue whales.

8. _____ milk does a baby whale drink?

It drinks 100 gallons of its mother's milk each day.

9. _____ weight does the baby whale gain?

A baby whale gains eight pounds each hour!

12 Practice

Complete the conversation with *how, how long, how many/much, how often,* **and** *how far.*

1. Man: Passport, please. _____*How*_____ are you today, ma'am?

Woman: I'm fine, thanks. And you?

2. Man: Fine. _____ was your trip?

Woman: Fine, thanks.

3. Man: _____ did you stay out of the country?

Woman: Not long. About three weeks.

4. Man: _____ countries did you visit?

Woman: Two countries: England and France.

5. Man: _____ do you go to Europe?

Woman: About once a year to visit friends.

6. Man: _____ friends do you have in Europe?

Woman: I have one friend in Oxford and one in Paris.

7. Man: _____ is Oxford from London?

Woman: It's about 50 miles, or 80 kilometers.

8. Man _____ have you known this friend?

Woman: I have known her for eight years.

9. Man: _____ money do you have on you?

Woman: I have about 200 dollars.

10. Man: _____ gifts did you buy?

Woman: I bought about seven gifts.

Man: Can I see them?

13 What Do You Think?

1. Where is this conversation taking place?
2. Who is the man?
3. Who is the woman?

14 Practice

Write questions for which the underlined words are the answers. Use all wh- words: *who, what, where, when, why, which,* and *how.*

1. Lions live in <u>Africa and Asia</u>.

   Where do lions live?

2. Lions live in groups. There are <u>about six to 30 lions</u> in a group.

   _____

3. <u>The male lion</u> is the largest member of the cat family.

   _____

4. A male lion can weigh <u>up to 520 pounds (240 kilos)</u>.

   _____

5. Lions eat <u>other animals</u>.

   _____

6. The male lion sleeps for <u>about 20</u> hours a day.

   _____

7. Sometimes the male can go without food <u>for a week</u>.

   _____

8. The job of the male lion is to <u>make sure other lions do not come near the home of his family</u>.

   _____

9. Sometimes the male lion makes a loud roar or sound. You can hear the sound <u>five miles</u> away.

   _____

10. <u>The female</u> lion kills other animals for food.

    _____

11. She takes the food to <u>the home of the family</u>.

    _____

12. The female lions usually hunt <u>at night</u>.

    _____

13. <u>The female lion</u> takes care of the baby lions.

    _____

14. Lions are in danger <u>because people kill them for sport</u>.

    _____

Practice

Write questions for which the underlined words are the answers. Use all wh- words.

1. Bob is an accountant.

   What is Bob?

2. He lives near Boston, in the United States.

   _____

3. He travels to work by subway.

   _____

4. His wife's name is Donna.

   _____

5. They have two children.

   _____

6. The girl is three.

   _____

7. The boy is nine.

   _____

8. Bob plays with the children after work.

   _____

9. He likes football and baseball. He prefers football.

   _____

10. He watches football on television because he doesn't have time to play.

    _____

11. His son watches it with him.

    _____

12. His son plays football at school.

    _____

13. He usually watches cartoons with his daughter.

    _____

14. Donna and Bob take the children out on Sundays.

    _____

15. Donna and Bob love their children.

    _____

Practice

Work with a partner. Make suggestions to visit three places in your city. Suggest the days and times you can both go. Use *how about* and *what about* to make suggestions.

Example:

You:	How about going to the park on Saturday?
Your partner:	OK. That's a good idea. What time?
You:	How about 10:30?
Your partner:	OK.

7f Tag Questions

Form

He's your brother, **isn't he?**

1. Tag questions are short questions at the end of a sentence. We form tag questions with the auxiliary verb from the first part of the sentence. The subject of the tag question at the end is always a pronoun—we do not repeat the noun. When we write, we always use a comma before the tag question.

   CORRECT: John is your brother, **isn't he?**
   INCORRECT: John is your brother, isn't ~~John~~?

2. We make a tag question in the same way we make a regular question, but when the main sentence is positive, the tag question is usually negative.

   He is a farmer, **isn't he?**

3. When the first part of the sentence is negative, the tag question is usually positive.

   He isn't a businessman, **is he?**

4. When the verb in the first part of the sentence is in the simple present or the simple past of any verb except *be*, we use the auxiliaries *do, does,* or *did* in the tag question. When the verb in the first part of the sentence is *be*, we use *be* again in the tag.

AFFIRMATIVE VERB, NEGATIVE TAG		NEGATIVE VERB, AFFIRMATIVE TAG	
Main Sentence	Tag	Main Sentence	Tag
She **likes** music,	**doesn't she?**	He **doesn't like** fish,	**does he?**
You **are** a student,	**aren't you?**	You **didn't** do it,	**did you?**
She**'s** learning English,	**isn't she?**	He **wasn't** nice to you,	**was he?**
We **had** fun,	**didn't we?**	We **didn't have** fun,	**did we?**

Note: With the subject and verb *I am,* the tag question is *aren't I* or *am I not*.

CORRECT: I'm late, **aren't I?**
INCORRECT: I'm late, ~~amn't~~ I?
CORRECT (very formal):   I'm late, **am I not?**

Function

1. We use tag questions when we want to check something we have said in the first part of the sentence.

    He lives in Utah, **doesn't he?** (The speaker is not sure and uses a tag question to check.)

2. We also use tag questions when we ask for agreement.

    The food is good, **isn't it?** (The speaker expects the answer "Yes.")
    You aren't angry, **are you?** (The speaker expects the answer "No.")

17 Practice

Match the sentences with the tag questions.

___d___ **1.** It gets very cold in the winter,   **a.** didn't he?

_____ **2.** You can't run that far,   **b.** does he?

_____ **3.** He got the job,   **c.** couldn't she?

_____ **4.** She could do it again,   **d.** doesn't it?

_____ **5.** He doesn't like opera,   **e.** were you?

_____ **6.** You weren't late,   **f.** can you?

18 Practice

Complete the conversation with the correct tag questions and short answers.

Tina: You went to Brazil, _____*didn't you?*_____
1

Jenny: Yes, I _____
2

Tina: They speak Portuguese there, _____
3

Jenny: Yes, they _____
4

Tina: You speak Portuguese, _____
5

Jenny: No, I _____
6

Tina: It was difficult to get around then, _____
7

Jenny: No, it _____ I spoke English.
8

Tina: A lot of people speak English there, _____
9

Jenny: Many people in hotels and restaurants do.

Tina: Rio is beautiful, _____
10

Jenny: Yes, _____
11

Tina: You had gone there before, _____
12

Jenny: Yes, a long time ago. You've been to Brazil, _____
13

Tina: No, I _____
14

7g Phrasal Verbs

Nick is **sitting down.**
He hasn't **picked up** the phone.

1. Many verbs in English consist of more than one word. These verbs have a verb plus a particle (an adverb such as *up or down*). These are phrasal verbs.

2. Sometimes we can guess the meaning of a phrasal verb.

   She walked into the room and **sat down.**
   When the president came into the room, everyone **stood up.**

   The phrasal verb *sit down* means "position yourself on a chair." The phrasal verb *stand up* means "get on your feet from a sitting position."

3. Many phrasal verbs have special meanings, for example:

   We **looked up** the words we didn't understand.

   The phrasal verb *look up* means "find information in a dictionary, encyclopedia, etc."

4. Some phrasal verbs do not take objects. In grammar, we call these intransitive phrasal verbs. Others do take objects. We call these transitive phrasal verbs.

   These two phrasal verbs do not take objects. They are intransitive.

Subject	Phrasal Verb
We	**sat down** at the table.
They	**stood up** to sing the national anthem.

These two phrasal verbs take objects. They are transitive.

Subject	Phrasal Verb	Object
I	**looked up**	**your number.**
The children	**put on**	**their coats.**

Practice

Underline the phrasal verbs in these sentences. If there is an object, circle it.

1. Please <u>turn on</u> the (radio).
2. We told the dog to lie down.
3. I have a cold. I can't get over it.
4. She took off her coat and sat down.
5. What time do you get up in the morning?

7h Intransitive Phrasal Verbs

Form / Function

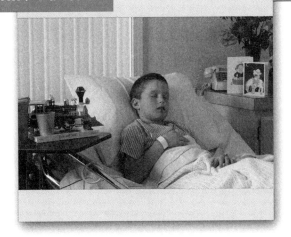

He's in the hospital.
He's **lying down.**

Here are some common phrasal verbs that are intransitive—they do not take objects.*

Phrasal Verb	Meaning	Example
break down	to stop working (as a machine)	My car has **broken down** three times this month.
get back	to return	They **got back** from Seoul yesterday.
get up	to arise from bed; to arise from a sitting position	We **got up** late this morning.
lie down	to rest in a horizontal position	I have a headache. I'm going to **lie down.**
set out	to leave (on a trip)	The boys **set out** at 6:00 A.M.
sit down	to sit on a chair	You should **sit down** in a job interview.
stand up	to arise from a sitting position	You should **stand up** when you meet someone.
stay up	to keep awake	We **stayed up** late to watch a movie.

*Some of these phrasal verbs can take objects, but the meaning is different. Like other verbs, phrasal verbs can have several meanings.

20 Practice

Complete the paragraph with phrasal verbs from the list.

got back   lay down   set out   stood up
got up   sat down   stayed up

This morning, we _____*set out*_____ for Silver Mountain. The night before,
                        1

we _____ late to get everything ready. In the morning, we
                2

_____ at 7:00. We walked for four hours before we _____
        3   4

to rest. We were tired. Julia was so tired that she _____ on the ground.
                                                              5

Finally, we _____ and continued our walk. When we got to the top of the
                    6

mountain, it was beautiful! Going back home was easier, and we _____ in
                                                                        7

time for dinner.

21 Practice

Complete the conversation with the correct phrasal verb in parentheses. Use the
correct form of the phrasal verb.

Karen: I feel so tired!

Jenny: ___*Sit down*___ for a few minutes. Why are you so tired? (stay up/sit down)
                1

Karen: I _____ until midnight last night. (stay up/break down)
                    2

Jenny: Why so late?

Karen: Because I didn't _____ from the library until then.
                                    3
          (set out/get back)

Jenny: Well, when did you _____ this morning? (lie down/get up)
                                        4

Karen: At 7:00. Then I had to walk to school.

Jenny: Why?

Karen: Because my car _____ two blocks from my house.
                                    5
          (break down/set out)

Jenny: Oh no! Maybe you shouldn't sit down. Maybe you should _____!
                                                                            6
          (set out/lie down)

Tell your partner about a difficult day that you have had. Use some phrasal verbs without objects.

Example:
As soon as I got up, I knew that it would be a terrible day. I set out for work and discovered that my car had broken down.

7i Transitive Phrasal Verbs: Separable

Form / Function

Susan's **looking up** a fact on the Internet.
She's **looking** it **up.**

Many transitive phrasal verbs—phrasal verbs that have objects—can have their objects in two different positions. We call these *separable* phrasal verbs because the object can separate the verb from the particle. Separable phrasal verbs are very common in English.

1. If a separable phrasal verb has a noun object, the object can come before or after the particle.

Subject	Verb	Particle	Noun Object	Particle
We	**turned**	**on**	the television.	
We	**turned**		the television	**on.**

2. If the object is a pronoun (*me, you, him, her, us, it, them*), the object must come between the verb and the particle.

Subject	Verb	Pronoun Object	Particle
We	**turned**	it	**on.**

CORRECT: We turned **it on.**
INCORRECT: We turned ~~on it.~~

3. Here are some common separable phrasal verbs.

Phrasal Verb	Meaning	Example
call back	to call someone on the phone after he/she has called you	**Call** me **back** when you can.
fill out	to complete a form or questionnaire	You should **fill** this form **out** for the doctor.
find out	to find information about something	I **found** the answer **out** when I talked to my teacher.
look up	to find information in a dictionary, telephone book, encyclopedia, etc.	I need to **look up** the capital of Botswana.
pick up	to lift someone/something	Please **pick** the baby **up**.
put off	to delay something to a later date	We should **put** the party **off** for a week.
put on	to wear something	**Put** your sweater **on** before you go out.
put down	to put something on a surface like the floor or a table	I **put** your box **down** on the kitchen counter.
take off	to remove clothes from the body	It's hot in here. I'm going to **take off** my coat.
turn on	to start a machine	Please **turn** the oven **on**.
turn off	to stop a machine	I can't hear you. **Turn** the radio **off**.
throw out/away	put something into the garbage or trash	I accidentally **threw** my homework **out**.
wake up	stop somebody from sleeping	I **woke up** the baby.
write down	write something on a piece of paper	I **wrote** the directions **down**, but now I can't find them.

23 Practice

Complete the sentences with the correct phrasal verb from the list.

call back   put down   turn off
fill out   put off   turn on
find out   put on   wake up
look up   take off   write down
pick up   throw out

1. My eyes are open at six every morning, but I _wake up_ my husband at 6:30.

2. Then I take a shower and _____ my clothes _____.

3. I _____ the television to listen to the news.

4. Before I leave, I _____ the television _____.

5. When I get to the office, I _____ my coat.

6. I _____ my bag on the floor, next to my desk.

7. Then, I _____ the phone.

8. I listen to my calls and _____ important messages _____ on a note pad.

9. When a person says it's urgent and gives me a number, I _____ the person _____.

10. I read all the mail. I _____ letters that I don't want.

11. I don't pay the bills immediately. I _____ some of them _____.

12. Sometimes I _____ a questionnaire. I think it's fun.

13. I can't remember numbers, so I _____ phone numbers _____ all the time.

14. At 4:00 in the afternoon, I call home and _____ what my teenagers are doing.

24 Practice

Write answers using separable phrasal verbs and pronouns.

1. What do you do with a form or questionnaire?

   I fill it out.

2. What do you do with old papers or things you do not want anymore?

   _____

3. What do you do with your shoes, shirt, or pants before you go to bed?

   _____

4. What do you do when a baby is crying in her bed?

   _____

5. What do you do with the television, faucet, or light?

7j   Transitive Phrasal Verbs: Inseparable

Amanda **ran into** Jane yesterday.

1. Some transitive phrasal verbs with objects cannot have an object between the verb and the particle. We call these *inseparable* phrasal verbs. The object can only go after the verb and the particle.

    CORRECT: Amanda **ran into** Jane yesterday.
    INCORRECT: Amanda ran ~~Jane into~~ yesterday.

2. There are fewer inseparable phrasal verbs than separable phrasal verbs. Here are some common ones.

Phrasal Verb	Meaning	Example
come across	to find by chance	How did you **come across** that book?
get into	to enter a car/taxi	We're late! **Get into** the car and let's go!
get off	to leave a bus/train/plane	Where do we **get off** the bus?
get on	to enter a bus/train/plane	Here's the bus. Let's **get on** it.
get out	leave a car/taxi	We're there. Let's **get out** of the car.
get over	to recover	She has **gotten over** the flu.
go over	to review	Be sure to **go over** phrasal verbs before the test!
look after	to take care of	I have to **look after** the children today.
look into	to investigate	The police are **looking into** the accident.
run into	to meet by chance	I **ran into** an old high school friend yesterday.

25 Practice

Complete the sentences with the correct phrasal verb from the list. Use the correct tense of the phrasal verb.

get into   get on   get over   look into
get off   get out   look after

Last night, Jackie had a problem with her bank account, and she needed to

_____look into_____ it. She stayed up until 11:30 P.M. This morning she got up
      1

very late! She quickly _____ a taxi and went to work. When she
                2

_____ of the taxi she felt dizzy. She was trying to _____
    3   4

a bad cold that she had had for a week. She told the people at the office she was going

home. She did not want to go out for a few days until she was better. She said her

husband could _____ her when she was at home. To _____ and
                5   6

_____ a bus in this cold weather was not going to help her get better.
   7

26 Practice

Write complete answers to these questions.

1. What are some kinds of transportation you get on and off?

   You get on and off buses and trains.

2. What are some forms of transportation you get into and out of?

   _____

3. What are some things or people you look after?

   _____

4. What are some illnesses that you have gotten over?

   _____

5. Tell about someone you have run into on the street.

   _____

6. What topics have you looked into for your classes?

   _____

Some of these sentences have errors in the use of phrasal verbs. If a sentence has an error, rewrite it correctly. If it does not have an error, write "Correct." Some of the phrasal verbs are separable and some are inseparable.

1. Let's put the meeting off until 2:00 this afternoon.

   Correct

2. This glass is broken. I'm going to throw out it.

   This glass is broken. I'm going to throw it out.

3. Sarah had a bad cold, but she got over it quickly.

   _____

4. You should put on your gloves before you go outside.

   _____

5. The baby was sleeping, but the phone woke up her.

   _____

6. I want to go the directions over before we start the trip.

   _____

7. What a beautiful painting! Where did you come across it?

   _____

8. Can you look some sales numbers up for Mr. Clark?

   _____

9. My brother called me this morning. I need to call back him.

   _____

10. Charles ran an old friend into this morning.

   _____

11. Here's the questionnaire. Fill out it in ink, please.

   _____

WRITING: Write a Questionnaire

Write questions about games or customs.

Step 1. Work with a partner. You want to find out what other people know about a topic such as the Olympic games or a custom in your country. Use the question words and forms you have learned in this unit to write a questionnaire with 20 questions.

Examples:
What are the Olympic games?
Which country will host the Olympic games next time?
When will the Olympic games be held?
Which Olympic sport is your country good at?

Step 2. Evaluate your questionnaire. For more writing guidelines, see pages 199–203.

Checklist

_____ Did you write 20 questions?

_____ Are all of your questions about the same general topic?

_____ Do you know the answer to each question?

_____ Are your questions clear?

Step 3. Edit your questions. Work with a partner or your teacher to edit the questions. Correct spelling, punctuation, vocabulary, and grammar.

Step 4. Make copies of your questionnaire. Ask people to write their answers. Report the results to the class.

SELF-TEST

A   Choose the best answer, A, B, C, or D, to complete the sentence. Mark your answer by darkening the oval with the same letter.

1. I can't study with the television on. Could you _____?

   A. turn off it   Ⓐ Ⓑ Ⓒ Ⓓ
   B. turn on it
   C. turn it off
   D. turn off television

2. If you don't know the meaning of the word, _____ in the dictionary.

   A. look up it   Ⓐ Ⓑ Ⓒ Ⓓ
   B. look it up
   C. look out it
   D. look the word

3. Sue: _____ did you live in Texas?
   Tom: Three years.

   A. When   Ⓐ Ⓑ Ⓒ Ⓓ
   B. How many
   C. What time
   D. How long

4. Sue: _____ didn't you write?
   Tom: Because I didn't have your address.

   A. Why   Ⓐ Ⓑ Ⓒ Ⓓ
   B. What
   C. How
   D. Which

5. He never eats broccoli, _____?

   A. doesn't he   Ⓐ Ⓑ Ⓒ Ⓓ
   B. eats he
   C. isn't he
   D. does he

6. Tom: _____ is that bird?
   Sue: It's an eagle.

   A. Which   Ⓐ Ⓑ Ⓒ Ⓓ
   B. What
   C. How
   D. Who

7. You haven't seen my keys, _____?

   A. did you   Ⓐ Ⓑ Ⓒ Ⓓ
   B. you have
   C. don't you
   D. have you

8. Joe: _____ wake me up at 7:00?
   Anne: Yes, I will.

   A. Will you   Ⓐ Ⓑ Ⓒ Ⓓ
   B. Would you
   C. Can you
   D. Could will

9. _____ going?

   A. What are you   Ⓐ Ⓑ Ⓒ Ⓓ
   B. Where you are
   C. Where are you
   D. Where you

10. Billy: _____ crying?
    Susie: No, I'm not.

    A. You are   Ⓐ Ⓑ Ⓒ Ⓓ
    B. Why are you
    C. You
    D. Are you

B Find the underlined word or phrase, A, B, C, or D, that is incorrect. Mark your answer by darkening the oval with the same letter.

1. How <u>many</u> does <u>it</u> <u>take</u> <u>to drive</u> to New
      A   B   C   D
   York from here?

   Ⓐ Ⓑ Ⓒ Ⓓ

2. <u>Did</u> they <u>came</u> <u>back</u> from <u>their</u> vacation?
     A   B   C   D

   Ⓐ Ⓑ Ⓒ Ⓓ

3. We <u>don't</u> <u>always</u> <u>have to</u> communicate
         A   B   C
   with words, <u>have</u> we?
                   D

   Ⓐ Ⓑ Ⓒ Ⓓ

4. We <u>have</u> apple pie <u>and</u> cherry pie. <u>What</u>
        A   B   C
   kind <u>would you</u> like?
            D

   Ⓐ Ⓑ Ⓒ Ⓓ

5. Here is <u>a form</u>. You <u>have to</u> fill in <u>it</u> and
             A   B   C
   give <u>it</u> to the passport control officer.
          D

   Ⓐ Ⓑ Ⓒ Ⓓ

6. I can't remember <u>the things</u> I <u>have to</u> do
                       A   B
   every day, so I write down <u>them</u> <u>on</u> a
                                 C   D
   piece of paper.

   Ⓐ Ⓑ Ⓒ Ⓓ

7. They <u>don't</u> have <u>any</u> children, <u>do</u> they
          A   B   C
   <u>have</u>?
     D

   Ⓐ Ⓑ Ⓒ Ⓓ

8. The weather report <u>didn't</u> say <u>anything</u>
                         A   B
   about rain today, <u>did</u> <u>he</u>?
                       C   D

   Ⓐ Ⓑ Ⓒ Ⓓ

9. You will <u>be</u> <u>back</u> <u>on</u> Monday as usual, <u>will</u>
              A   B   C   D
   you?

   Ⓐ Ⓑ Ⓒ Ⓓ

10. Brenda <u>was</u> very sick <u>with</u> a bad cold, but
              A   B
    now <u>she's</u> getting it <u>over</u>.
           C   D

    Ⓐ Ⓑ Ⓒ Ⓓ

APPENDICES

Appendix 1   Grammar Terms

Adjective
An adjective describes a noun or a pronoun.

My cat is very **intelligent**. He's **orange** and **white**.

Adverb
An adverb describes a verb, another adverb, or an adjective.

Joey speaks **slowly**. He **always** visits his father on Wednesdays.

His father cooks **extremely** well. His father is a **very** talented chef.

Article
An article comes before a noun. The definite article is *the*. The indefinite articles are *a* and *an*.

I read **an** online story and **a** magazine feature about celebrity lifestyles.

The online story was much more interesting than **the** magazine feature.

Auxiliary Verb
An auxiliary verb is found with a main verb. It is often called a "helping" verb.

Susan **can't** play in the game this weekend. **Does** Ruth play baseball?

Base Form
The base form of a verb has no tense. It has no endings (*–ed, –s,* or *–ing*).

Jill didn't **see** the band. She should **see** them when they are in town.

Comparative

Comparative forms compare two things. They can compare people, places, or things.

This orange is **sweeter than** that grapefruit.

Working in a large city is **more stressful than** working in a small town.

Conjunction

A conjunction joins two or more sentences, adjectives, nouns, or prepositional phrases. Some conjunctions are *and, but,* and *or.*

Kasey is efficient, **and** her work is excellent.

Her apartment is small **but** comfortable.

She works Wednesdays **and** Thursdays.

Contraction

A contraction is composed of two words put together with an apostrophe. Some letters are left out.

Frank usually **doesn't** answer his phone.   (doesn't = does + not)

He's really busy.   (he's = he + is)

Does he know what time **we're** meeting?   (we're = we + are)

Imperative

An imperative gives a command or directions. It uses the base form of the verb, and it does not use the word *you.*

Go to the corner and **turn** left.

Modal

A modal is a type of auxiliary verb. The modal auxiliaries are *can, could, may, might, must, shall, should, will,* and *would.*

Elizabeth **will** act the lead role in the play next week.

She **couldn't** go to the party last night because she had to practice her lines.

She **may** be able to go to the party this weekend.

Noun

A noun is a person, an animal, a place, or a thing.

My **brother** and **sister-in-law** live in **Pennsylvania**. They have three **cats**.

Object

An object is the noun or pronoun that receives the action of the verb.

Georgie sent **a gift** for Johnny's birthday.

Johnny thanked **her** for the gift.

Preposition

A preposition is a small connecting word that is followed by a noun or pronoun. Some are a*t, above, after, by, before, below, for, in, of, off, on, over, to, under, up,* and *with.*

> Every day, Jay drives Chris and Ally **to** school **in** the new car.
> **In** the afternoon, he waits **for** them **at** the bus stop.

Pronoun

A pronoun takes the place of a noun.

> Chris loves animals. **He** has two dogs and two cats.
> His pets are very friendly. **They** like to spend time with people.

Sentence

A sentence is a group of words that has a subject and a verb. It is complete by itself.

Sentence: Brian works as a lawyer.
Not a sentence: Works as a lawyer.

Subject

A subject is the noun or pronoun that does the action in the sentence.

> **Trisha** is from Canada.
> **She** writes poetry about nature.

Superlative

Superlative forms compare three or more people, places, or things.

> Jennifer is **the tallest** girl in the class.
> She is from Paris, which is **the most romantic** city in the world.

Tense

Tense tells when the action in a sentence happens.

Simple present	–	The cat **eats** fish every morning.
Present progressive	–	He **is eating** fish now.
Simple past	–	He **ate** fish yesterday morning.
Past progressive	–	He **was eating** when the doorbell rang.
Future with *be going to*	–	He **is going to eat** fish tomorrow morning, too!
Future with *will*	–	I think that he **will eat** the same thing next week.

Verb

A verb tells the action in a sentence.

> Melissa **plays** guitar in a band.
> She **loves** writing new songs.
> The band **has** four other members.

Appendix 2   Irregular Verbs

Base Form	Simple Past	Past Participle	Base Form	Simple Past	Past Participle
be	was, were	been	keep	kept	kept
become	became	become	know	knew	known
begin	began	begun	leave	left	left
bend	bent	bent	lend	lent	lent
bite	bit	bitten	lose	lost	lost
blow	blew	blown	make	made	made
break	broke	broken	meet	met	met
bring	brought	brought	pay	paid	paid
build	built	built	put	put	put
buy	bought	bought	read	read	read
catch	caught	caught	ride	rode	ridden
choose	chose	chosen	ring	rang	rung
come	came	come	run	ran	run
cost	cost	cost	say	said	said
cut	cut	cut	see	saw	seen
do	did	done	sell	sold	sold
draw	drew	drawn	send	sent	sent
drink	drank	drunk	shake	shook	shaken
drive	drove	driven	shut	shut	shut
eat	ate	eaten	sing	sang	sung
fall	fell	fallen	sit	sat	sat
feed	fed	fed	sleep	slept	slept
feel	felt	felt	speak	spoke	spoken
fight	fought	fought	spend	spent	spent
find	found	found	stand	stood	stood
fly	flew	flown	steal	stole	stolen
forget	forgot	forgotten	swim	swam	swum
get	got	gotten/got	take	took	taken
give	gave	given	teach	taught	taught
go	went	gone	tear	tore	torn
grow	grew	grown	tell	told	told
hang	hung	hung	think	thought	thought
have	had	had	throw	threw	thrown
hear	heard	heard	understand	understood	understood
hide	hid	hidden	wake up	woke up	woken up
hit	hit	hit	wear	wore	worn
hold	held	held	win	won	won
hurt	hurt	hurt	write	wrote	written

Appendix 3   Spelling Rules for Endings

Adding a Final –s to Nouns and Verbs

Rule	Example	-s
1. For most words, add –s without making any changes.	book bet save play	books bets saves plays
2. For words ending in a consonant + *y*, change the *y* to *i* and add –es.	study party	studies parties
3. For words ending in *ch, s, sh, x,* or *z,* add –es.	church class wash fix quiz	churches classes washes fixes quizzes
4. For words ending in *o,* sometimes add –es and sometimes add –s.	potato piano	potatoes pianos
5. For words ending in *f* or *lf,* change the *f* or *lf* to *v* and add –es. For words ending in *fe,* change the *f* to *v* and add –s.	loaf half life	loaves halves lives

Adding a Final -ed, -er, -est, and -ing

Rule	Example	-ed	-er	-est	-ing
1. For most words, add the ending without making any changes.	clean	cleaned	cleaner	cleanest	cleaning
2. For words ending in silent e, drop the e and add -ed, -er, or -est.	save like nice	saved liked	saver nicer	 nicest	saving liking
3. For words ending in a consonant + y, change the y to i and add the ending. Do not change or drop the y before adding -ing.	sunny happy study worry	 studied worried	sunnier happier	sunniest happiest	 studying worrying
4. For one-syllable words ending in one vowel and one consonant, double the final consonant, then add the ending. Do not double the last consonant if it is a w, x, or y.	hot run bat glow mix stay	 batted glowed mixed stayed	hotter runner batter	hottest	 running batting glowing mixing staying
5. For words of two or more syllables that end in one vowel and one consonant, double the final consonant if the final syllable is stressed.	begin refer occur permit	 referred occurred permitted	beginner		beginning referring occurring permitting
6. For words of two or more syllables that end in one vowel and one consonant, do NOT double the final consonant if the final syllable is NOT stressed.	enter happen develop	entered happened developed	developer		entering happening developing

Appendix 4   Capitalization Rules

First words

1. Capitalize the first word of every sentence.

    They live in San Francisco.   **W**hat is her name?

2. Capitalize the first word of a quotation.

    She said, "**M**y name is Nancy."

Names

1. Capitalize names of people, including titles of address.

    Mr. **T**hompson   **A**lison **E**mmet   **M**ike **A**. **L**ee

2. Capitalize the word "I".

    Rose and **I** went to the market.

3. Capitalize nationalities, ethnic groups, and religions.

    Latino   **A**sian   **K**orean   **I**slam

4. Capitalize family words if they appear alone or with a name, but not if they have a possessive pronoun or article.

    He's at **A**unt Lucy's house.   vs.   He's at an **a**unt's house.

Places

1. Capitalize the names of countries, states, cities, and geographical areas.

    Tokyo   **M**exico   the **S**outh   **V**irginia

2. Capitalize the names of oceans, lakes, rivers, and mountains.

    the **P**acific **O**cean   **L**ake **O**ntario   **M**t. **E**verest

3. Capitalize the names of streets, schools, parks, and buildings.

    Central **P**ark   **M**ain **S**treet   the **E**mpire **S**tate **B**uilding

4. Don't capitalize directions if they aren't names of geographical areas.

    She lives **n**ortheast of Washington. We fly **s**outh during our flight.

Time words

1. Capitalize the names of days and months.

    Monday   **F**riday   **J**anuary   **S**eptember

2. Capitalize the names of holidays and historical events.

    Christmas   **I**ndependence **D**ay   **W**orld **W**ar I

3. Don't capitalize the names of seasons.

    spring   **s**ummer   **f**all   **w**inter

Titles

1. Capitalize the first word and all important words of titles of books, magazines, newspapers, and articles.

    The Sound and the Fury *Time Out* *The New York Times*

2. Capitalize the first word and all important words of titles of films, plays, radio programs, and TV shows.

    Star Wars "Friends" *Mid Summer Night's Dream*

3. Don't capitalize articles (*a, an, the*), conjunctions (*but, and, or*) and short prepositions (*of, with, in, on, for*) unless they are the first word of a title.

    The Story of Cats *The Woman in the Dunes*

Appendix 5   Punctuation Rules

Period

1. Use a period at the end of a statement or command.

    I live in New York. Open the door.

2. Use a period after most abbreviations.

    Ms. Dr. St. U.S.

    Exceptions: NATO UN AIDS IBM

3. Use a period after initials.

    Ms. K.L. Kim F.C. Simmons

Question Mark

1. Use a question mark at the end of questions.

    Is he working tonight? Where did they use to work?

2. In a direct quotation, the question mark goes before the quotation marks.

    Martha asked, "What's the name of the street?"

Exclamation Point

Use an exclamation point at the end of exclamatory sentences or phrases. They express surprise or strong emotion.

    Wow! I got an A!

Comma

1. Use a comma to separate items in a series.

    John will have juice, coffee, and tea at the party.

2. Use a comma to separate two or more adjectives that each modify the noun alone.

    Purrmaster is a smart, friendly cat. (*smart* and *friendly* cat)

3. Use a comma before a conjunction (*and, but, or, so*) that separates two independent clauses.

    The book is very funny, and the film is funny too.

    She was tired, but she didn't want to go to sleep.

4. Don't use a comma before a conjunction that separates a sentence from an incomplete sentence.

    I worked in a bakery at night and went to class during the day.

5. Use a comma after an introductory clause or phrase.

    After we hike the first part of the trail, we are going to rest.

6. Use a comma after *yes* and *no* in answers.

    Yes, that is my book.

    No, I'm not.

7. Use a comma to separate quotations from the rest of a sentence. Don't use a comma if the quotation is a question and it is in the first part of the sentence.

    The student said, "I'm finished with the homework."

    "Are you really finished**?**" asked the student.

Apostrophe

1. Use apostrophes in contractions.

    don't (*do not*)   it's (*it is*)   he's (*he is*)   we're (*we are*)

2. Use apostrophes to show possession.

    Anne's book (the book belongs to Anne)

Quotation Marks

1. Use quotation marks at the beginning and end of exact quotations. Other punctuation marks go before the end quotation marks.

    Burt asked, "When are we leaving?"

    "Right after lunch," Mark replied.

2. Use quotation marks before and after titles of articles, songs, stories, and television shows. Periods and commas are usually placed before the end quotation marks, while question marks and exclamation points are placed after them. If the title is a question, the question mark is placed inside the quotation marks, and appropriate punctuation is placed at the end of the sentence.

Burt's favorite song is "Show Some Emotion" by Joan Armatrading.

He read an article called "Motivating Your Employees."

We read an interesting article called "How Do You Motivate Employees?".

Italics and Underlining

1. If you are writing on a computer, use italic type (*like this*) for books, newspapers, magazines, films, plays, and words from other languages.

Have you ever read *Woman in the Dunes*?

How do you say *buenos dias* in Chinese?

2. If you are writing by hand, underline the titles of books, newspapers, magazines, films, and plays.

Have you ever read <u>Woman in the Dunes</u>?

How do you say <u>buenos dias</u> in Chinese?

Appendix 6   Writing Basics

1. Sentence types

There are three types of sentences: declarative, interrogative, and exclamatory. Declarative sentences state facts and describe events, people, or things. We use a period at the end of these sentences. Interrogative sentences ask yes/no questions and wh- questions. We use a question mark at the end of these sentences. Exclamatory sentences express surprise or extreme emotion, such as joy or fear. We use an exclamation point at the end of these sentences.

2. Indenting

We indent the first line of a paragraph. Each paragraph expresses a new thought, and indenting helps to mark the beginning of this new thought.

3. Writing titles

The title should give the main idea of a piece of writing. It should be interesting. It goes at the top of the composition and is not a complete sentence. In a title, capitalize the first word and all of the important words.

4. Writing topic sentences

The topic sentence tells the reader the main idea of the paragraph. It is always a complete sentence with a subject and a verb. It is often the first sentence in a paragraph, but sometimes it is in another position in the paragraph.

5. Organizing ideas

Information can be organized in a paragraph in different ways. One common way is to begin with a general idea and work toward more specific information. Another way is to give the information in order of time using words like *before, after, as, when, while,* and *then*.

6. Connecting ideas

It is important to connect the ideas in a paragraph so that the paragraph has cohesion. Connectors and transitional words help make the writing clear, natural, and easy to read. Connectors and transitional words include *and, in addition, also, so, but, however, for example, such as, so ... that,* and *besides*.

7. The writing process

Success in writing generally follows these basic steps:

❖ Brainstorm ideas.
❖ Organize the ideas.
❖ Write a first draft of the piece.
❖ Evaluate and edit the piece for content and form.
❖ Rewrite the piece.

Index

yes/no questions, 20–21
Probably, 60
Pronouns, 109–28
    indefinite, 121, 123–24
    possessive, 113–14
    quoted/reported speech, 110–11
    reflexive, 115–16

Q

Questions
    phrasal verbs, 179–81, 183–84, 186
    tag questions, 177–78
    wh-
        past progressive tense, 39
        present perfect tense, 131
        present progressive tense, 21
        simple past tense, 35
        simple present tense, 21
    yes/no
        future tense, 57, 59
        past perfect progressive tense, 153
        past perfect tense, 149
        past progressive tense, 39, 47
        present perfect progressive tense, 144
        present perfect tense, 131
        simple past tense, 30, 35, 47
        simple present tense, 20–21

R

Rarely, 6–7
Recently, 132
Reflexive pronouns, 115–16

S

See, 17–18
Seldom, 6–7
Separable phrasal verbs, 183–84
-S/-es, 2, 80–81
She, 110–11, 115–16
Should, 161
Simple past tense, 29–54
    affirmative/negative statements, 30, 34, 47
    consonants, 31
    -ed, 30–31, 34
    irregular verbs, 34–35
    and past progressive tense, 42–47
    past time clauses, 44–45
    present perfect tense and, 142
    wh- questions, 35
    yes/no questions, 30, 35, 47
Simple present tense, 1–27
    action/nonaction verbs, 17–18
    adverbs of frequency, 6–7
    affirmative/negative statements, 2–3
    consonants, 2
    future tense/future time, 67
    irregular verbs, 3

and present progressive tense, 13, 17–18
    -s/-es, 2
    wh- questions, 21
    yes/no questions, 20
Since, 131, 136, 145
Singular nouns, 2, 80–81, 86, 91
Some, 90–92, 121
Someone/somebody/something/somewhere,
123–24
Sometimes, 6–7
Spelling
    of -s and -es, 2, 80–81
    verbs ending in -ing, 9–10, 39, 144–45,
    153–54
Statements. *See* Affirmative/negative statements
Subject pronouns, 110–11
Subjects
    nouns as, 84
    who/what as, 166

T

Tag questions, 177–78
Tenses. *See* Future tense; Past perfect progressive
tense; Past perfect tense; Past progressive tense;
Present perfect progressive tense; Present perfect
tense; Present progressive tense; Simple past
tense; Simple present tense
The, 100, 102
Themselves, 115–16
They/them/theirs, 110–11, 115–16, 121
Think, 16
Time clauses, 44–45, 71–72
Time expressions, 64, 67, 136, 145
Transitive verbs, 186

U

Us, 110–11
Used to/used to have, 46–47, 256
Usually, 6–7

V

Verbs
    action/nonaction, 17–18
    auxiliary, 160–61, 163–64
    ending in -ing, 9–10, 39, 144–45, 153–54
    gerunds, 173
    intransitive, 181
    irregular, 3, 34–35
    nonprogressive, 15–16, 43
    nouns as objects of, 84
    participles, 144
    past participles, 130–31, 138, 140, 149–50
    phrasal, 179–81, 183–84, 186
    seeing/hearing, 17–18
    transitive, 186
-Ves, 81
Vowels, 80–81

W

Y